VALUE INVESTING
&
BEHAVIORAL FINANCE

Vivek Choudhary

To my Mentor My Hero Warren Edward Buffett, Charles Thomas Munger, Philip Arthur Fisher, Kenneth Jeffrey Marshall, Benjamin Graham, Peter Lynch & Parag Parikh.

PREFACE

"Arise, awake, and stop not until the goal is achieved."

- Swami Vivekananda

I believe Passion and determination is very important in achieving our life goal.

Take up one idea. Make that one idea your life - think of it, dream of it, and live on that idea. Let the brain, muscles, nerves, every part of your body, be full of that idea, and just leave every other idea alone. This is the way to success.

-Swami Vivekananda

Value investing is my passion and I am happy to find my passion in my early days in high school when I come across a physical share certificate. I find it very interesting and wish to learn how investing works.

My first shares certificate I saw was ITC (India Tobacco Company Limited), My father subscribes IPO 1990, from that day still we are having the stock with us,

The CAGR is 22.5%. We are holding the share for 50 Years and still with me that the power of compounding and it's all happened because ITC is having Durable competitive Advantage and Strong Moat around it. We have never seen Technical Chat or graph of the company; all we were interested in knowing if the company is strong and have a product that customer is willing to buy even when company increase price and beat inflation.

I learn value investing and started reading about Warren Buffett and I read and read, today I read 150 pages daily, I love reading and I believe words of Charlie Munger...

Value investing is an investment strategy that involves picking stocks that appear to be trading for less than their intrinsic or book value. Value investors actively ferret out stocks they think the stock market is underestimating.

"In my whole life, I have known no wise people, who didn't read all the time -- none, zero. You'd be amazed at how much Warren reads--and at how much I read. My children laugh at me. They think I'm a book with a couple of legs sticking out."
― Charles T. Munger, Poor Charlie's Almanack: The Wit and Wisdom of Charles T. Munger

In this book I have shared the value invested process and discipline, this Process has created wealth in this field of investment. I am using this process and I understand how value investing work, and I wish each and every one should create wealth from this proven process and discipline.

Value investing is a long-term investment and I believe Value Investing is easy to learn but be in Discipline can be difficult when the rest of the world seems to be selling and you are buying, in the stock market is how you behave will make you wealthy. Your becoming wealthy is determined by your ability to stay in the market and asking yourself why this opportunity is only for me & Reason to be a Value Investor.

Value Investor on average perform greater than growth stock, you want to be in winning team with extraordinary investors like warren buffet and that looks to be a very good team to be in.

The quality of the company is very important to have Moats, should be within circle of competence, and keep a Margin of Safety. I intend to buy and sell never.

I try to have written clear & simple so that anyone can easily understand and use the process of value investing and behavioral finance. I hope this book will serve your purpose and create wealth in your life.

Introduction

"Rule No. 1: Never lose money. Rule No. 2: Never forget rule No.1"

— **Warren Buffett**

This book is design how to use Value Investing? You buy something which is below the value, stock that is out of favour. The business owned by ethical management, which has moat around it, business which require least capital, require less amount of debts, have margin of safety and must be within Circle of Competence.

It is most successful Process Principal and discipline Framework developed by great investor Benjamin Graham is regarded by many to be the father of value investing. Along with David Dodd, he wrote Security Analysis, first published in 1934.

This book is a study of Benjamin Graham, Warren Buffett, Peter Lynch, Charles Thomas Munger & Philip Arthur Fisher, Parag Parikh, the investment Principal shared by them.

What you will learn –

- How to use value Investing?
- How to use 72 formulas?
- How to Create Wealth?
- Why Compound interest is 8 wonders of the world?
- Why investors find risky when prices are low?
- How a company creates Value to shares holders?
- How to Manage Risk?
- Do financial Behaviour is important?
- Does the investor make different type of decision?
- Is all investor rational?
- Able to create value investing model.
- Learn to create a Circle of Competence.
- Understand rational investment decisions.
- Learn to Analyses Security as per value investing Process, Discipline, and Principal Framework.
- Learn Competitive Advantage & Moat.
- Learn how your behaviour can create wealth for you.

This Book Divide in Eight Module Introduction to Value Investing, Understanding the Business, Financial Performance & Growth, Strategic analysis using

Competitive advantage & Moat, understanding Management Integrity and Rationality like ownership, dividend, share repurchase, Inside Purchase: going forward we read Margin of Safety & Valuation such as EV to EBITDA, MCAP/FCF, MCAP/BV, PEG Ratio and last we will read about Behavioral finance, how we should be rational in investing.

About the Authors

Vivek Choudhary is a Value Investor & Entrepreneur who has over 20 years of experience in investment and entrepreneurship. Involve in diversify business Commodities, Manufacturing, Hotel & Automobiles.

He earned MBA in finance & Marketing at IIPM, MDP in Strategic Market Planning at IIM, Equity Research Analyst at BSE Institute, Value Investing at Stanford University Continue studies, and Entrepreneurship Essential & Leading with Finance at HBX Harvard Business School & Value Investing at Columbia Business School, Business Lesson Cohort at Harvard Business School Online.

He is passionate about Value Investing and invests globally. His hobby is reading. He reads every day value investing books and finance books.

He admires his Hero Mr Warren Buffett Chief Executive Officer of Berkshire Hathaway – He follows his footprint of Value Investing. For him reading and studying are like compounding, it will help him in achieving his passion.

He wrote the book

- **Value Investing & Behavioral Finance**

- **Stock Investing & Financial Statement Analysis**

- **Value Investing - Legendary Graham & Dodd Valuation**

- **Value Investing CHECKLIST**

- **Why Investors Fail in Stock Market**

- **Billionaires Mind -Business Plan**

CONTENTS

Preface   III

Introduction   VII

Module 1

Introduction to Value Investing

- Value Investing and Growth Investing   9
- Diversification   14
- Risk   19
- Compound Interest & Rule 72   28
- Accounting is a language of business   38
- The Purpose of Financial Statement   40
- Income Statement   42
- Balance Sheet   44
- Cash Flow Statement   46
- Free Cash Flow   47
- Capital Employed   49

CONTENTS

Module 2

Understanding the Business   51

Company Background: Company Ticker symbol   62

, Name, Founded Year, Founder & History

, Headquarters, Industries Served, Current CEO,

Employee, Revenue, Profit, Product   Details

, Product   wise Revenue %, Customer Details

, Product wise Customer, Main Competitors

Geographic areas served & Revenue   wise %

Create Circle of Competence   69

CONTENTS

Module 3

Financial Performance & Growth

- Gross Profit Margin — 77
- Operating Profit Margin — 78
- Net Profit Margin — 79
- Return on Equity — 80
- DuPont Ratio — 82
- Growth in Earnings Per Share — 88
- Growth in Book Value Per Share — 90
- Return on Capital Employed — 92
- Free Cash Flow Return on Capital Employed — 94
- Total Liabilities-to-Equity ratio — 95

CONTENTS

Module 4

Competitive Advantage 97

Porter's Five Forces

- Threat of new entrants 99
- Threat of substitutes 100
- Bargaining power of customers 101
- Bargaining power of suppliers 102
- Competitive Rivalry 103

Understanding Moat 109

Creating an Economic Moat
- Intangible assets 117
- Customer Switching Costs 118
- Cost advantage 119
- Efficient Scale 120
- Network Effect 121

CONTENTS

Module 5

Strategic Analysis 124

SWOT Analysis
- Strengths 127
- Weaknesses 128
- Opportunities 129
- Threats 130

BCG Matrix 139

- Dogs 142
- Question marks 143
- Stars 144
- Cash cows 144

CONTENTS

Module 6

Management Integrity and Rationality 151

- Compensation & Owners   155
- Share Repurchases   158
- Dividends   163
- Inside Purchase   165
- Related Party Transactions   166

Module 7

Margin of Safety 168

Valuation

- EV to EBITDA   174
- MCAP/FCF   179
- MCAP/BV   181
- PEG Ratio   184

CONTENTS

Module 8

Behavioral Finance 188

Standard Finance vs Behavioral finance 193

Efficient Market Hypothesis (EMH) 197

- Weak Form EMH 198
- Smi-Strong Form EMH 199
- Strong Form EMH 200

Prospect Theory 203

Cognitive Bias

- Cognitive biases 216

Overcoming Behavioral Finance Issues 223

VALUE INVESTING & BEHAVIOURL FINANCE

Module 1

Introduction to Value Investing

Why value Investing?

"A stock is not just a ticker symbol or an electronic blip; it is an ownership interest in an actual business, with an underlying value that does not depend on its share price."
— *Benjamin Graham, the Intelligent Investor*

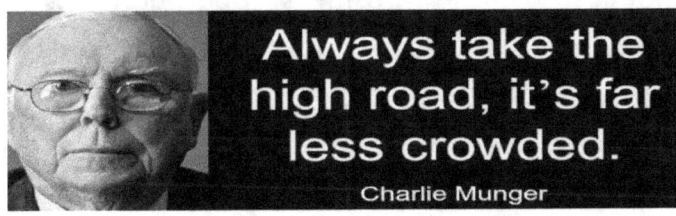

Benjamin Graham, Warren Buffett and Charlie Munger. Graham is the third from left.

"An investment operation is one which, upon thorough analysis, promises safety of principal and an adequate return. Operations not meeting these requirements are speculative."

— Benjamin Graham, the Intelligent Investor

Value Investing is of guiding principles, Process that combine two critical ingredients to be successful in value investing, A good understanding of the economics of the business operations with a disciplined valuation approach. Approaching investment Decisions, do we want to buy this company or not? Do we want to become partners with the rest of the shareholders or not? You buy something which is below the value, stock that is out of favour. The business owned by ethical management, which has a moat around it, business which require the least capital, require less number of debts, have a margin of safety, and must be within Circle of Competence.

This strategy began primarily with Benjamin Graham, a professor and professional investor in the early 20th century. He created a thorough guide that focused on the company's cash flows, the ability to pay the debt, future prospects, and other factors in order to arrive at a valuation of the company.

The idea is that the market might either misunderstand a company or undervalue its true earning potential. By looking at the business fundamentals, a savvy investor can estimate what a company is actually worth regardless of where the market sets its price. Once you find a company that is being undervalued based on its operations, you can invest in the low market price. When the market figures out how much it is actually worth, the stock price will increase.

The investment paradigm which we know of as value investing derives from the investment ideas of Benjamin Graham (1894-1976) and his David Dodd (1895-1988), both from Columbia Business School. Since then, value investing has taken many forms, but they all include the basic idea of buying good-quality securities at knock-down prices, buying stocks that are intrinsically worth $1 for just 50 cents. Stock prices can change owing to several reasons, underlined by a popularised market tendency which causes a share's price to waver from its intrinsic value.

In other words, value investors seek companies with long-term potential but temporary downtrends in share prices due to market biases. Such investors analyse several parameters financial metrics to determine which company is performing below its capacity in the market.

The concept started to take off in a serious way after Graham's and Dodd's text 'Security Analysis' was published in 1931.

Value investing allows you to reinvest a dividend for a higher profit potential over time. Compounding at, say 3%, can significantly impact your wealth as you retire. Compounding will result in more earnings in a shorter period without the need for extra work on your part.

Value investing is all about finding secret sales on stocks and buying them at lower prices.

Approaches to investment

Long term

Fundamental
Value

Levels
Market Value Vs Value of stock

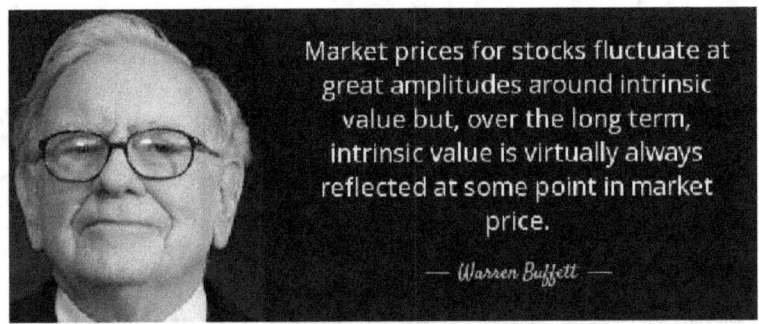

> Market prices for stocks fluctuate at great amplitudes around intrinsic value but, over the long term, intrinsic value is virtually always reflected at some point in market price.
> — *Warren Buffett*

There is a significant difference between intrinsic value and market value, though both are ways of valuing a company. Intrinsic value is an estimate of the actual true value of a company, regardless of market value. Market value is the current value of a company as reflected by the company's stock price. **Value Investing is easy to learn but be in Discipline** can be difficult when the rest of the world seems to be selling and you are buying, in the stock market is how you behave will make you wealthy.

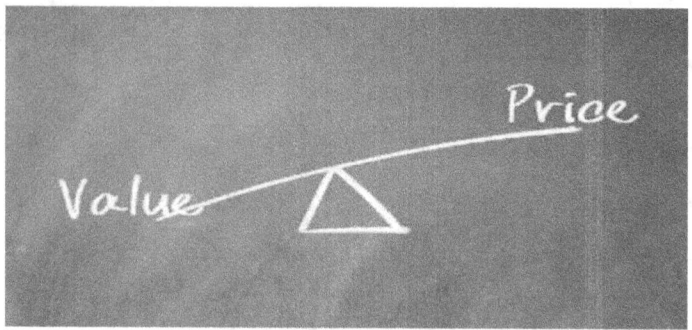

One other thing Mr. Market doesn't mind if you don't pay any attention to him. He shows up to work every day— rain, sleet, or snow— ready and willing to sell you his half of the business, the price depending entirely on his mood. You are free to ignore him or take him up on his offer. Regardless of what you do, he will be back tomorrow with a new quote.

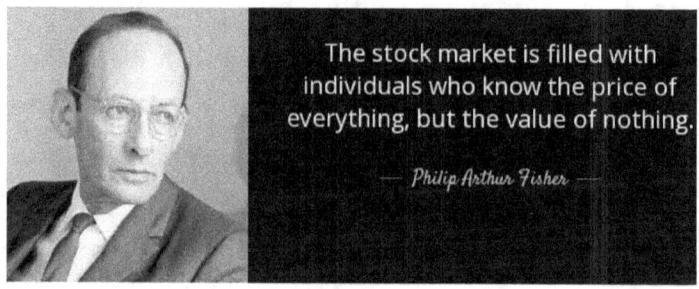

The stock market is filled with individuals who know the price of everything, but the value of nothing.

— Philip Arthur Fisher —

Value Investing is to value a stock for higher performance in long term investment, to become a value investor you need to Discipline and Patience. Holding your position for a long period of time, your becoming wealthy is determined by your ability to stay in the market and asking yourself why this opportunity is only for me.

The Value investing Process is understanding the company, thinking as you buying whole or potion of the company, the company is not only a stock ticker, there is a story behind every stock. You need to search for the story, do research, manage risk, and trust yourself.

The Three Principal of Value Investing

- Mr. Market
- The circle of competence
- Margin of Safety

Reason to be a Value Investor

Value Investor on average performs greater than growth stock, you want to be in winning team with extraordinary investors like Warren Buffett and that looks to be a very good team to be in. To begin with, the most important term that you probably need to know about value investing is 'intrinsic value'. It, in simple terms, is the true value that stock holds in the market. There are times when market conditions, global trends, and other factors lead to a drop in the stock prices below this intrinsic value. A value investor looks for these opportunities where the stocks of a trustable, high-value company go down because of market conditions.

Since value investing focuses on putting our money in a stock which is at a low, the chances of further suffering price depreciation are much lower as compared to investing in normally- priced stocks. If a stock has an intrinsic value of Rs 100 and is currently trading at Rs 60, then the Rs 40 difference is a surety that you will make more profits than someone who has bought the stock at its value. This is called the margin of safety and is a key contributor in value stocks making more profits.

The key to value investing is not falling for the bandwagon effect. If there is a stock that a majority of people are investing in, then a value investor will avoid it! Stepping away from the herd mentality has been the key reason that value investors like Warren Buffet have created wealth. The focus of a value investor is to understand the true value of a stock and investing in it when everyone else is ignoring it.

Value Investing and Growth Investing

Growth and value are two fundamental approaches, or styles, in stock and stock mutual fund investing. Growth investors seek companies that offer strong earnings growth while value investors seek stocks that appear to be undervalued in the marketplace.

Growth investing

Growth investors are attracted to companies that are expected to grow faster (either by revenues or cash flows, or definitely by profits) than the rest. As growth is the priority, companies reinvest earnings in themselves in order to expand, in the form of new workers, equipment, and acquisitions.

Don't expect dividends from growth companies—right now it's go big or go home. Growth companies offer higher upside potential and therefore are inherently riskier. There's no guarantee a company's investments in growth will successfully lead to profit. Growth stocks experience stock price swings in greater magnitude, so they may be best suited for risk-tolerant investors with a longer time horizon.

Value investing

Value investing is about finding diamonds in the rough—companies whose stock prices don't necessarily reflect their fundamental worth. Value investors seek businesses trading at a share price that's considered a bargain. As time goes on, the market will properly recognize the company's value and the price will rise.

Additionally, value funds don't emphasize growth above all, so even if the stock doesn't appreciate, investors typically benefit from dividend payments. Value stocks have more limited upside potential and, therefore, can be safer investments than growth stocks.

Value Investing

- Investing in companies that are undervalued in the stock market.
- Value stocks trade at a low or discounted price.
- Low-level of risk.

Growth Investing

- Investing in companies that have generated higher than average returns in current times.
- Growth stocks trade at a high price.
- High-level of risk.

With value investing we have reason to believe that the strategy may work, even before we see any data. This is for a few reasons. First of all, cheaper is often better. As Warren Buffett often points out, when socks are on sale, it can be a good time to buy socks rather than run of out the store. The same can be true of stocks, if a particular stock is on sale in terms of trading at a cheaper price relative to its earnings, then maybe it's a good time to buy it.

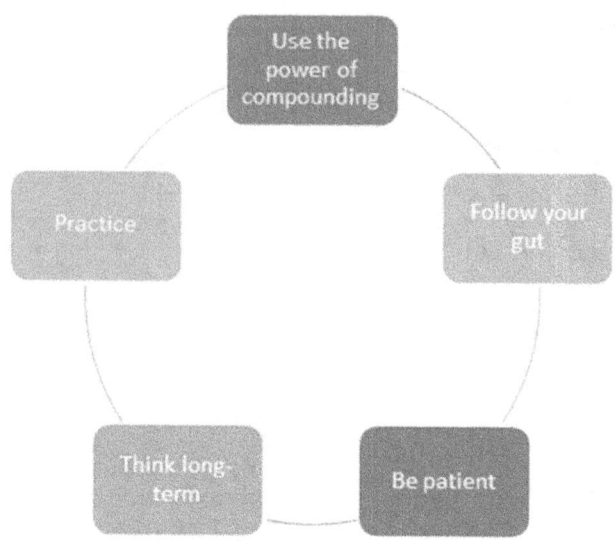

Intrinsic value is an equivalent concept to the Net Worth. When evaluating businesses, intrinsic value can be hard to arrive at. As investors are removed from the day-to-day operations of the company, they are necessarily reduced to making assumptions about asset uses and values. They may also make back-of-the-envelope estimates for future earnings and revenues. Even if an investor has access to greater detail of the financial position than what the company is required to disclose to the public any projections or future estimates will likely vary from the eventual results. As a result, investors tend to use certain key financial ratios to arrive at a valuation that is "close enough". A value investor also realizes that valuation and analysis is necessarily not an exact science. There are many ways errors can be introduced in the process, and some of these errors might have disproportionate effect on the intrinsic value calculation. As a result, the value investor is advised to learn towards conservatism in assumptions. Read more about estimating the intrinsic value of a company

After all, it is also possible that the intrinsic value of the company may fall. The reasonable confidence that the company will remain profitable in the near future, it is very likely that the intrinsic value of the company will not decline, and only grow. A growing intrinsic value should in the long run cause an increase in the stock price. However, keep in mind that companies may be able to show an accounting profit even as in reality the business may be running losses, at least in the short run. It is best to adjust the accruals to cash basis where possible to get a true picture of the business fundamentals. Cash flow analysis becomes critical.

Diversification

The main reason used to justify diversification is that it spreads risk. In other words, if your portfolio contains only shares and the stock market falls, then you will sustain large losses.

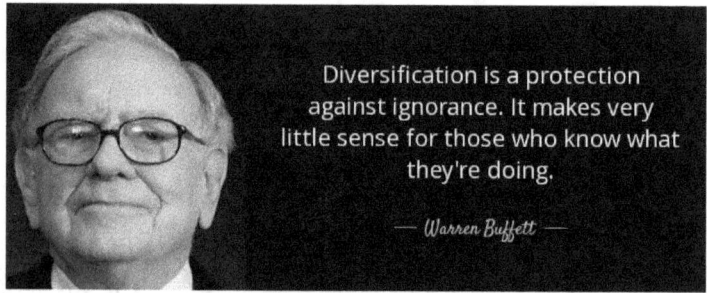

In finance, diversification is the process of allocating capital in a way that reduces the exposure to any one particular asset or risk. A common path towards diversification is to reduce risk or volatility by investing in a variety of assets. If asset prices do not change in perfect synchrony, a diversified portfolio will have less variance than the weighted average variance of its constituent assets, and often less volatility than the least volatile of its constituents.

What Buffett "diversification" is a portfolio with 50% in 3 stocks and another 30% in about 8 stocks. By today's standards, this portfolio would be considered intensely focused and not at all diversified.

COMPANY	% Of Portfolio
APPLE INC	30%
BANK AMER CORP	13%
COCA COLA CO	9%
AMERICAN EXPRESS CO	8%
WELLS FARGO & CO NEW	7%
KRAFT HEINZ CO	4%
JPMORGAN CHASE & CO	3%
US BANCORP DEL	3%
MOODYS CORP	2%

Mr. Buffett has changed nothing in the investing years; however, Billionaire investor Warren Buffett famously stated that "diversification is protection against ignorance. It makes little sense if you know what you are doing." In Buffet's view, studying one or two industries in great depth, learning their ins and outs, and using that knowledge to profit on those industries is more lucrative than spreading a portfolio across a broad array of sectors so that gains from certain sectors offset losses from others.

He calls what your fund manager is doing buying 100 stocks a vast "over-diversification" that is sure to result in mediocre returns, returns that are less than the market itself because of your fund manager's fees.

In his 1993 annual letter to shareholders, Warren Buffett writes:

"Portfolio concentration may well decrease risk if it raises, as it should, both the intensity with which an investor thinks about a business and the comfort-level he must feel with its economic characteristics before buying into it."

"If you are a know-something investor, able to understand business economics and to find five to ten sensibly-priced companies that possess important long-term competitive advantages, conventional diversification makes no sense for you. It is apt simply to hurt your results and increase your risk."

Warren Buffett, Letter to Shareholders, Berkshire Hathaway (1993).

The idea of excessive diversification is madness."

Diversification can lessen risk for most investors. Yet for those who put in the time and work to thoroughly understand their investments, Munger believes they will earn the highest returns possible by investing only in their best ideas.

Warren Buffet Strategy

Stick With Long Term Value Investing Strategies

Don't let fear and greed change your investing criteria and values. Avoid being overwhelmed by outside forces that affect your emotions. Never sell into panic.

Invest in What You Understand

Buffet only invests in companies he understands and believes have stable or predictable products for the next 10 – 15 years. This is why he has typically avoided technology companies.

Invest Like You Are Buying the Entire Company

Treat investing in a stock as though you are buying the entire company. I always take a hard look at enterprise value because this is the total price of a company. In other words, it is the price you would be paying for the company if you could buy the whole company at current prices.

Companies with Competitive Advantages

Companies with pricing power, strategic assets, powerful brands, or other competitive advantages have the ability to outperform in good and challenging times. A long-term investing strategy requires investing in companies that can whether both good and bad economic times.

Find Quality Companies

Buffet believes in quality investing. He would rather pay a fair price for a great company than a low price for a mediocre company.

Keep Cash on Hand

Investment opportunities become available through broad market corrections or individual stocks that become bargains. These are not predictable events; so, cash on hand is an important concept in value investing.

Require a Margin of Safety

Purchasing stocks with a margin of safety below their intrinsic value reduces risk and provides an allowance for unforeseen negative events.

Compounding and Patience

Buffet believes in long term value investing because he understands the power of exponential growth. Companies with sustainable profits can pay and grow their dividends. There are few more powerful long term investing strategies than dividend growth compounding.

Risk

According to modern portfolio theory, risk can be divided into two elements: systematic risk and unsystematic risk.

Systematic Risk

Systematic risk – also called undiversifiable risk or market risk – is the risk inherent in the overall market and is not specific to a particular stock or industry. This type of risk is both unpredictable and impossible to completely avoid. It cannot be mitigated through diversification.

Unsystematic Risk

Unsystematic risk – also called nonsystematic risk, specific risk, diversifiable risk, or residual risk – is the company- or industry-specific risk that is inherent in each investment. This type of risk can be reduced through diversification. By owning stocks in different companies, different industries, and different types of assets and securities, investors can be less affected by an event or decision that has a strong impact on any single asset.

If you own only one stock, then the systematic and unsystematic risk in your one stock portfolio is very high. The stock market could tank (systematic risk) or your company could lose a key customer (unsystematic risk).

But if you own 100 stocks – like you might if you own an index fund – then the systematic risk in your 100 stock portfolios is unchanged but your unsystematic risk is almost zero, so the overall risk is lower. Yes, the stock market could still tank (systematic risk), but if one single company loses a key customer (unsystematic risk) – or even goes bankrupt – then your entire portfolio would only be slightly affected.

Famous value investor Seth Klarman of the Baupost Group wrote in Margin of Safety:

"I find it preposterous that a single number reflecting past price fluctuations could be thought to completely describe the risk in a security. Beta views risk solely from the perspective of market prices, failing to take into consideration specific business fundamentals or economic developments. The price level is also ignored, as if IBM selling at 50 dollars per share would not be a lower-risk investment than the same IBM at 100 dollars per share.

Beta fails to allow for the influence that investors themselves can exert on the riskiness of their holdings through such efforts as proxy contests, shareholder resolutions, communications with management, or the ultimate purchase of sufficient stock to gain corporate control and with it direct access to underlying value.

Beta also assumes that the upside potential and downside risk of any investment are essentially equal, being simply a function of that investment's volatility compared with that of the market as a whole. This too is inconsistent with the world as we know it. The reality is that past security price volatility does not reliably predict future investment performance (or even future volatility) and therefore is a poor measure of risk.

Warren Buffett and Beta

Graham-and-Doddsville, Warren had this to say about beta:

"I would like to say one important thing about risk and reward. Sometimes risk and reward are correlated in a positive fashion. If someone were to say to me, "I have here a six-shooter and I have slipped one cartridge into it. Why don't you just spin it and pull it once? If you survive, I will give you $1 million." I would decline — perhaps stating that $1 million is not enough. Then he might offer me $5 million to pull the trigger twice — now that would be a positive correlation between risk and reward!

The exact opposite is true with value investing. If you buy a dollar bill for 60 cents, it's riskier than if you buy a dollar bill for 40 cents, but the expectation of reward is greater in the latter case. The greater the potential for reward in the value portfolio, the less risk there is.

One quick example: The Washington Post Company in 1973 was selling for $80 million in the market. At the time, that day, you could have sold the assets to any one of ten buyers for not less than $400 million, probably appreciably more. The company owned the Post, Newsweek, plus several television stations in major markets. Those same properties are worth $2 billion now, so the person who would have paid $400 million would not have been crazy.

Now, if the stock had declined even further to a price that made the valuation $40 million instead of $80 million, its beta would have been greater. And to people that think beta measures risk, the cheaper price would have made it look riskier. This is truly Alice in Wonderland. I have never been able to figure out why it's riskier to buy $400 million worth of properties for $40 million than $80 million. And, as a matter of fact, if you buy a group of such securities and you know anything at all about business valuation, there is essentially no risk in buying $400 million for $80 million, particularly if you do it by buying ten $40 million piles of $8 million each.

"Risk to us is 1) the risk of permanent loss of capital, or 2) the risk of inadequate return." Risk has many different dimensions that must be considered including sources, magnitude, outcomes and decision-making inputs. In terms of a definition, Seth Klarman writes that risk is: "described by both the probability and the potential amount of loss." Charlie Munger emphasizes an important point in his quotation since it is the permanent loss which should be the focus of investors since temporary drops can actually represent an opportunity for an investor if they can purchase more of an asset at the lower price and ride out the drop in price. The focus of this definition of risk is on potential "outcomes." In terms of "sources" of risk, Warren Buffett believes that "risk comes from not knowing what you're doing" and that "the best way to minimize risk is to think." This is why Charlie Munger spends so much time thinking about thinking.

You shouldn't be imprisoned by volatility." "Some great businesses have very volatile returns – for example, See's usually loses money in two quarters of each year – and some terrible businesses can have steady results." Charlie Munger and Warren Buffett are very focused on finding investments which possess odds of success that are substantially in their favor. If the process of generating returns along the way is lumpy that is not only perfectly acceptable but it can be a significant financial advantage since others may be unwilling to do so creating mispriced assets that can be purchased at a bargain price. Howard Marks argues: "in order to achieve superior results, an investor must be able – with some regularity – to find asymmetries: instances when the upside potential exceeds the downside risk. That's what successful investing is all about."

We don't give a damn about lumpy results. Everyone else is trying to please Wall Street. This is not a small advantage." Munger is pointing out that buying what is unpopular or requires a long-term viewpoint tends to be underpriced. Since buying underpriced assets creates a margin of safety, it lowers risk and increases financial returns. On volatility, Ben Graham once wrote: "A serious investor is not likely to believe that the day-to-day or month-to-month fluctuations of the stock market make him richer or poorer…

This great emphasis on volatility in corporate finance we regard as nonsense. Let me put it this way; as long as the odds are in our favour and we're not risking the whole company on one throw of the dice or anything close to it, we don't mind volatility in results. What we want are favourable odds." Charlie Munger has said that he is a "focus" investor since he is not a "know nothing" investor. In his personal accounts and fund, he manages he is not a believer in diversification. He is also careful to note that few people should invest like him and should instead buy a diversified portfolio of low-cost index funds. Warren Buffett's statement about what he and Charlie Munger do at Berkshire is as famous as it is succinct. "Take the probability of loss times the amount of possible loss from the probability of gain times the amount of possible gain.

"All investment evaluations should begin by measuring risk. This is said to involve incorporating an appropriate margin of safety, avoiding permanent loss of capital and insisting on proper compensation for risk assumed." If you decide to incur risk and face the possibility of loss or injury, you should insist on being paid for doing so. Munger is saying that the best way to manage investment risk is to buy assets at a price that reflects enough of a margin of safety that the outcome will be favourable even if you make a mistake.

Any person offers you a chance to earn lots of money without risk, don't listen to the rest of their sentence. Follow this and you'll save yourself a lot of misery." When it comes to investing it is wise to follow the advice of Howard Marks and think of the future as a probability distribution rather than some fixed outcome that is knowable or predictable in advance. Almost nothing about the future is certain except death and taxes. No one says it better than Howard Marks when it comes to risk: "not being able to know the future doesn't mean we can't deal with it. It's one thing to know what's going to happen and something very different to have a feeling for the range of possible outcomes and the likelihood of each one happening. Saying we can't do the former doesn't mean we can't do the latter."

The power of Value Investing

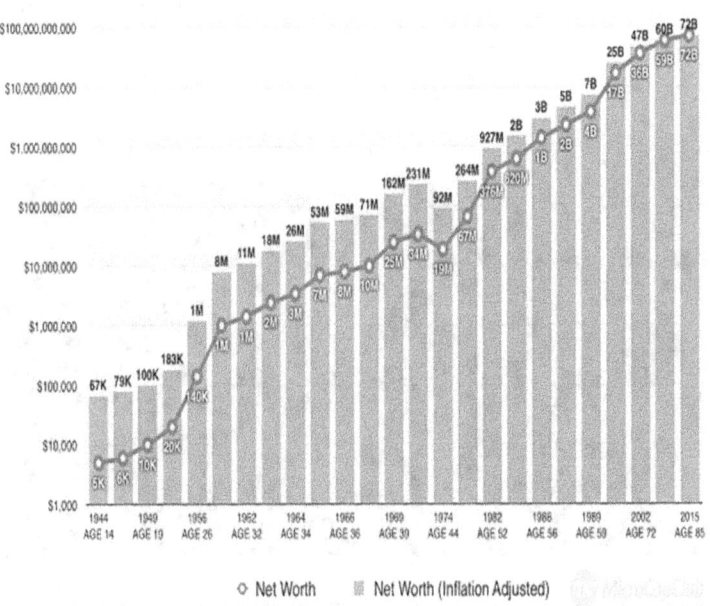

The Return will be determined by:

- You're Behaviour.
- Your character.
- Your temperament.
- To stay in the market when others are leaving the market.

Compound Interest

Compound interest is such a powerful yet neglected idea, that Albert Einstein famously called it "the eighth wonder of the world. He, who understands it, earns it ... he who doesn't ... pays it." Buffett bought his first stock at 11, but has earned 99 percent of his wealth since his 50th birthday.

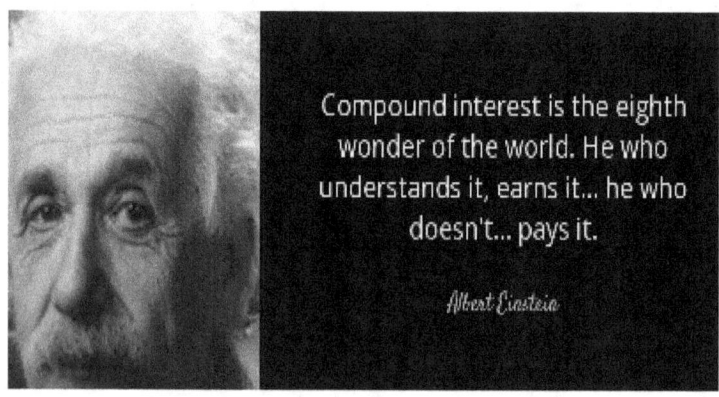

The concept of compound interest is that interest is added back to the principal sum so that interest is gained on that already-accumulated interest during the next compounding period.

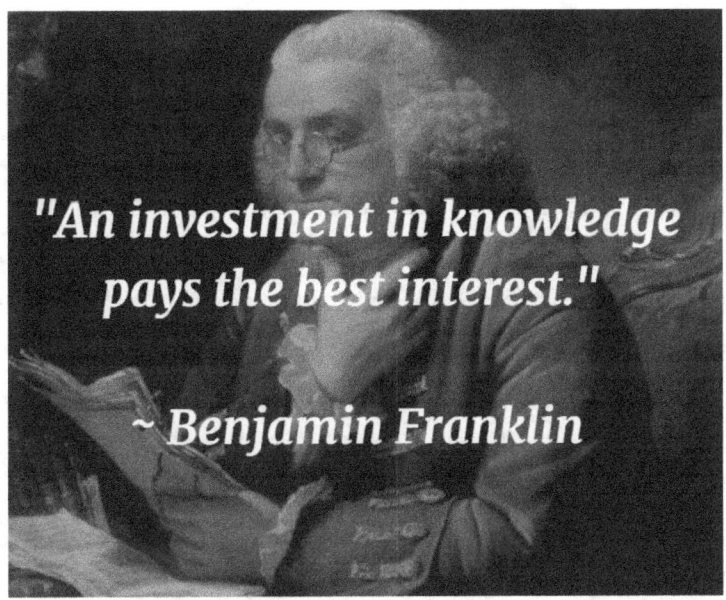

Compound interest is the addition of interest to the principal sum of a loan or deposit, or in other words, interest on interest. It is the result of reinvesting interest, rather than paying it out, so that interest in the next period is then earned on the principal sum plus previously accumulated interest. Compound interest is standard in finance and economics.

Compound interest is contrasted with simple interest, where previously accumulated interest is not added to the principal amount of the current period, so there is no compounding. The simple annual interest rate is the interest amount per period, multiplied by the number of periods per year. The simple annual interest rate is also known as the nominal interest rate.

Interest calculated on the initial principal, which also includes all of the accumulated interest of previous periods of a deposit or loan. Thought to have originated in 17th century Italy, compound interest can be thought of as "interest on interest," and will make a sum grow at a faster rate than simple interest, which is calculated only on the principal amount.

When you invest, interest is calculated for the first period (be it a month or a year). This interest is then added to the original total. Following on from that, the interest for the next period is calculated but is based on the gross figure from the first period.

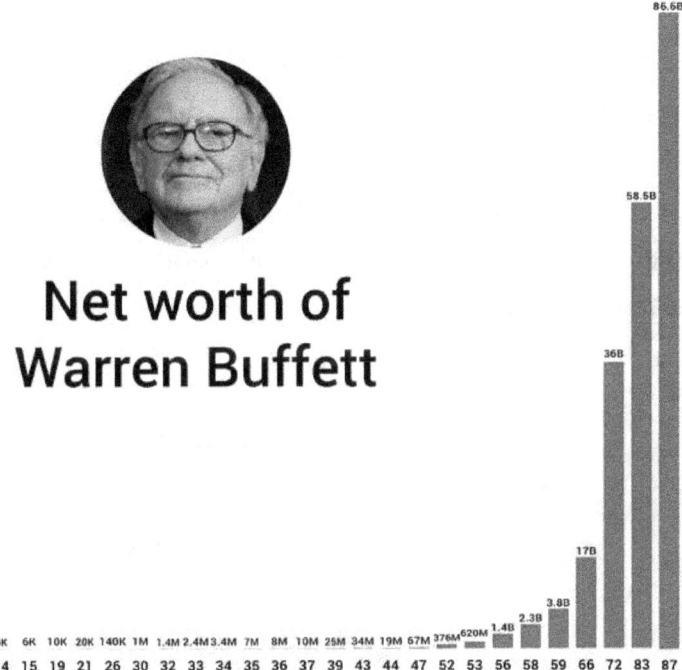

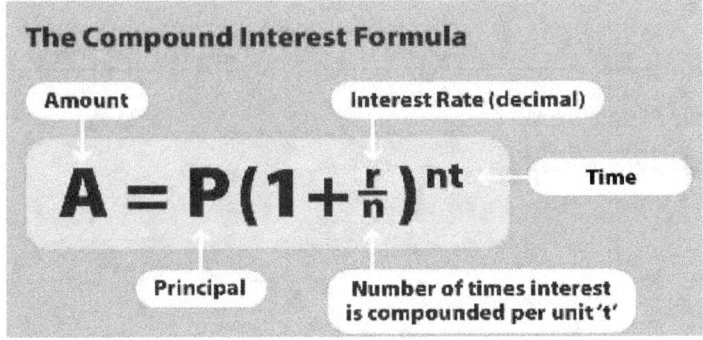

To give a graphical example, the graph below shows the result of $1000 invested over 20 years at an interest rate of 10%. The principal figure is in green. The blue part of the graph shows the result of 10% interest without compounding. Finally, the purple part demonstrates the benefit of compound interest over those 20 years.

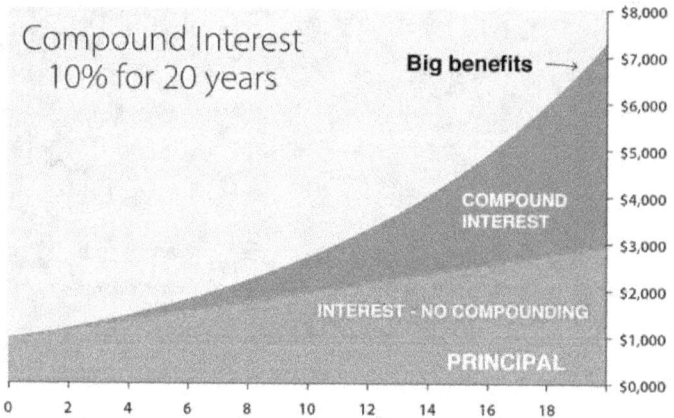

"The most powerful force in the world is compound interest"
– Albert Einstein

Example

How to be a millionaire using compound interest and practice Value Investing.

If you start with $ 10,000.00 in a stock earning a 20% interest rate, compounded an annually, and make 10,000.00 deposits on an Annual basis, after 16 Years your investment will have grown to 1,073,879.24 -- of which 170,000.00 is the total of your beginning balance plus deposits, and 903,879.24 is the total interest earnings.

It will be $ 1 Million.

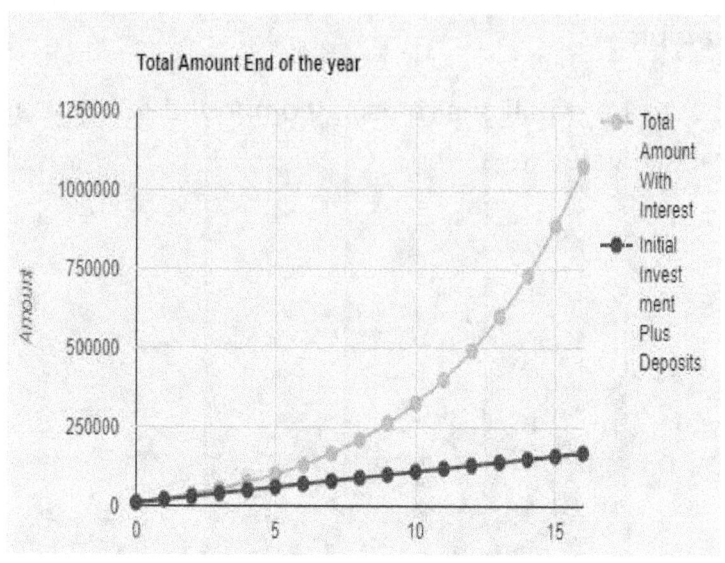

Amount showing through PieChart

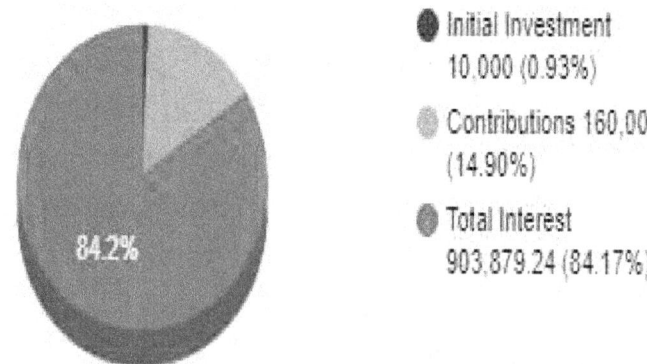

- Initial Investment 10,000 (0.93%)
- Contributions 160,000 (14.90%)
- Total Interest 903,879.24 (84.17%)

The Rule of 72

The **Rule of 72** is a great mental math shortcut to estimate the effect of any growth rate, from quick financial calculations to population estimates. Here's the formula:

Years to double = 72 / Interest Rate

Interest Rate = 72 / Year

If an investment scheme promises an 8% annual compounded rate of return, it will take approximately (72 / 8) = 9 years to double the invested money. Note that a compound annual return of 8% is plugged into this equation as 8, and not 0.08, giving a result of nine years

Warren Buffett is he best-known value investor today, this course shares with you a model. This is useful because it's the perspective that delivers the highest returns overtime. In this Module we will cover all the aspect of business.

In this, we will be asking.

- Do Mr. Market Rational?
- Do I understand business?

- Do Business is within my circle of competence?
- Does the business have good performance growth & Moats?
- Is it available at below intrinsic value, have a margin of safety? Can we be Rational?

This question will guide to find the best company to invest, if we don't understand the business, we should stop analysing the company and if we understand business, we can move further. Value investors use financial analysis, don't follow the herd, and invest for long-term of quality companies.

We will be reading Annual Report; an annual report is a comprehensive report on a company's activities throughout the preceding year. Annual reports are intended to give shareholders and other interested people information about the company's activities and financial performance. They may be considered as grey literature.

Annual reports will include:

General corporate information

Operating and financial review

Director's Report

Corporate governance information

Chairpersons statement

Auditor's report

Contents: non-audited information

Financial statements, including

Balance sheet also known as Statement of Financial Position

Income statement also profit and loss statement.

Statement of changes in equity

Cash flow statement

Notes to the financial statements

Accounting policies

We will be reading United States companies, annual report known as a 10K and poxy Statement Pursuant to Section 14(a) Executive Compensation Program, us accounting principle is Generally Accepted Accounting Principles and for India we will be reading Annual Report.

Accounting is a Language of Business

The phrase "accounting is the language of business" is attributed to Warren Buffet.

Accounting is often called the "Language of business." It is a means of communicating information about a business. Its responsibility is applying a thorough knowledge of the theory of accounting, that is, generally accepted principles of accounting to the practical field of business in order that income and financial position may be stated fairly.

Accounting is the analysis and interpretation of book - keeping records. It includes not only maintenance of accounting records but also the preparation of financial and economical information which involves the measurement of transaction and other events pertaining to a business.

To operate a business profitably and to stay solvent, the profitability and solvency of a business should be measured at regular intervals. For that, it is essential to know whether a business is earning sufficient profits or incurring losses and it has sufficient money to pay off debts. Accounting provides all these pieces of information which enable the management to guide the business on a profitable and solvent course.

We express ourselves through our language. Similarly, the results of the activities are expressed through accounting with the help of financial statements. Accounting measures the performances of the business, that is, profitability and financial position. Thus, the language of accounting expresses the whole story of the undertaking through the various processes of accounting. The progress of the firm can easily be compared and seen with the help of various accounting data.

Financial records and accounting reports tell the story of how a company is doing financially, so it's no wonder that accounting is often referred to as the language of business. When executives and decision makers talk about their companies' health, they typically refer to financial statements. Income, expenses, debt and liabilities are all components of financial documents and must be understood by anyone wanting to communicate clearly in the business world but are ultimately a main factor toward success in the business world.

Investors use the information to determine whether they want to invest in a business. Accounting documents allow them to measure performance using ratios, such as inventory turnover, liquidity and stock performance. Without the knowledge of basic accounting principles, it is impossible to make smart decisions about investing.

The Purpose of Financial Statement

How to identify company with durable competitive advantage through financial statement, do company have unique product that help in increasing revenue.

Income statement, balance sheet and cash flow statement use to discover whether company will make you rich over time in long term investment as did with warren buffet.

It is critical for an investor to separate the daily short-term noise in the stock prices and concentrate on the underlying business performance. Over a long term, the stock prices of a fundamentally strong company tend to appreciate, thereby creating wealth for its investors.

Quality Company creates wealth for the shareholders such example such as Apple, Master Card, Visa, Bank of America, and Amazon, Berkshire Hathaway.

In Indian Market company create wealth such as Page Industries, Nestle India, HDFC Bank, TCS Limited, ITC.

These companies have delivered on an average over 20% compounded annual growth return (CAGR) year on year for over 10 years. To give you a perspective, at a 20%CAGR the investor would double his money in roughly about 3.5 years; this is the power of great fundamentally strong companies.

"Like Warren, I had a considerable passion to get rich, not because I wanted Ferraris – I wanted the independence. I desperately wanted it." - Charlie Munger

"It's far better to buy a wonderful company at a fair price than a fair company at a wonderful price." - Warren Buffett

A financial statement is a quantitative description of a business. We'll focus on three: income statement, cash flow statement, and balance sheet.

Income Statement

The Profit and Loss statement is also popularly referred to as the P&L statement, Income Statement, Statement of Operations, and Statement of Earnings. The Profit and Loss statement shows what has transpired during a time period. The P&L statement reports information on:

1. The revenue of the company for the given period (yearly or quarterly)

2. The expenses incurred to generate the revenues

3. Tax and depreciation

4. The earnings per share number

The Top Line of the company (Revenue)

You may have heard analysts talk about the top line of a company. When they do so, they are referring to the revenue side of the P&L statement. The revenue side is the first set of numbers the company presents in the P&L.

The Expense details

We had learnt about the revenues a company generates. Moving further on the P&L statement, in this chapter we will look at the expense side of the Profit and Loss Statement along with the associated notes. Expenses are generally classified according to their function, which is also called the cost of sales method or based on the nature of expense.

    Revenue
−   Cost of goods sold
−   Operating expenses
=   *Operating income*

+   Non-operating income
=   *Earnings before interest and taxes*

−   Interest expense
=   *Earnings before taxes*

−   Taxes
=   *Net income*

Remember almost all line items in the P&L statement will have an associated note. You can always look into the notes to seek greater clarity. Also, at this stage we have just understood how to read the P&L statement, but we still need to analyse what the numbers mean.

We will do this when we take up the financial ratios. Also, the P&L statement is very closely connected with the other two financial statements i.e the balance sheet and the cash flow statement. We will explore these connections at a later stage.

Balance Sheet

While an income statement and a cash flow statement both look at a business over a period of time, a balance sheet looks at a business at a single point in time. The balance sheet equation While the P&L statement gives us information pertaining to the profitability of the company, the balance sheet gives us information pertaining to the assets, liabilities, and the shareholders equity.

The balance sheet however is prepared on a flow basis, meaning, it has financial information pertaining to the company right from the time it was incorporated. Thus, while the P&L talks about how the company performed in a particular financial year; the balance sheet on the other hand discusses how the company has evolved financially over the years

Assets, both tangible and intangible are owned by the company. An asset is a resource controlled by the company, and is expected to have an economic value in the future. Typical examples of assets include plants, machinery, cash, brands, patents etc. Assets are of two types, current and non-current,. Liability on the other hand represents the company's obligation. The obligation is taken up by the company because the company believes these obligations will provide economic value in the long run. Liability in simple words is the loan that the company has taken and it is therefore obligated to repay back. Typical examples of obligation include short term borrowing, long term borrowing, payments due etc. Liabilities are of two types namely current and non-current in any typical balance sheet, the total assets of company should be equal to the total liabilities of the company.

Assets = Liabilities

The equation above is called the balance sheet equation or the accounting equation. In fact, this equation depicts the key property of the balance sheet i.e the balance sheet should always be balanced.

In other word the Assets of the company should be equal to the Liabilities of the company.

This is because everything that a company owns (Assets) has to be purchased either from either the owner's capital or liabilities.

Owners Capital is the difference between the Assets and Liabilities. It is also called the 'Shareholders Equity' or the 'Net worth'. Representing this in the form of an equation:

Shareholder's equity = Assets – Liabilities

Cash Flow Statement

The Cash flow statement is a very important financial statement, as it reveals how much cash the company is actually generating.

1. **Operational activity** (OA): Activities that are directly related to the daily core business operations are called operational activities. Typical operating activities include sales, marketing, manufacturing, technology upgrade, resource hiring etc

Net Profit - Interest Expenses - Income Tax = EBIT

Calculate the cash from operating activities as follows:

EBIT + Depreciation = Cash from Operating Activities

2. **Investing activities** (IA): Activities pertaining to investments that the company makes with an intention of reaping benefits at a later stage. Examples include parking money in interest bearing instruments, investing in equity shares, investing in land, property, plant and equipment, intangibles and other noncurrent assets etc

3. **Financing activities (FA):** Activities pertaining to all financial transactions of the company such as distributing dividends, paying interest to service debt, raising fresh debt, issuing corporate bonds etc

Free Cash Flow

Free Cash Flow Free cash flow is the cash a company produces through its operations, less the cost of expenditures on assets. In other words, free cash flow (FCF) is the cash left over after a company pays for its operating expenses and capital expenditures, also known as CAPEX.

The formula for free cash flow is:

Free Cash Flow = Operating Cash flow – Capital Expenditures

Definition: Free cash flow, or owner earnings as Warren Buffet likes to call it, is a measure of the company's ability to generate cash over a period of time. We like to say it is the money an owner could take out of his business and spend for his own benefit.

Owner earnings is a valuation method detailed by Warren Buffett in Berkshire Hathaway's annual report in 1986. He stated that the value of a company is simply the total of the net cash flows (owner earnings) expected to occur over the life of the business, minus any reinvestment of earnings.

Buffett defined owner earnings as follows:

"These represent (a) reported earnings plus (b) depreciation, depletion, amortization, and certain other non-cash charges...less (c) the average annual amount of capitalized expenditures for plant and equipment, etc. that the business requires to fully maintain its long-term competitive position and its unit volume.

Buffett because it gives a clearer view of a company's ability to generate positive cash flow. A positive Free Cash Flow means your company is actually generating surplus cash flow. Negative Free Cash Flow means your company is burning cash. What I love about Free Cash Flow is that it not only gives you an accurate view of your cash flow position, it also provides clues on how to improve it. It can help us understand what changes we can make to unlock more cash.

Capital Employed

Capital Employed has many definitions. In general, it is the capital investment necessary for a business to function. It is commonly represented as total assets less current liabilities, Capital employed can also refer to as the value of all the assets used by a company to generate earnings. By employing capital, companies invest in the long-term future of the company. Capital employed is helpful since it's used with other financial metrics to determine the return on a company's assets as well as how effective management is at employing capital. Capital investments include stocks and long-term liabilities. It also refers to the value of assets used in the operation of a business. In other words, it is a measure of the value of assets minus current liabilities. Both of these measures can be found on the balance sheet. A current liability is the portion of debt that must be paid back within one year. In this way, capital employed is a more accurate estimate of total assets.

Capital Employed is the total amount of investment made for running the business. It should not be confused with the term "Capital". "Capital" represents funds contributed by the owner (s) in a business, whereas "Capital Employed" has a wider meaning. It includes funds coming from both the owners and lenders, i.e., it covers both equity and debt.

Capital Employed = Total Assets – Current Liabilities
Formula

VALUE INVESTING & BEHAVIOURL FINANCE

Module 2

Understanding the Business

Buy a business, not its stock.

Treat a stock purchase as if you were buying the entire business, using the following.

Is the business simple and understandable from your perspective as an investor?

Do you understand how the company generates sales, incurs expenses, and produces profits?

That means you need to understand revenues, expenses, cash flow, labour relations, pricing, flexibility and capital requirements - an exceptionally high level of knowledge. It means that investors should buy shares only in companies within their own circle of financial and intellectual understanding. An investor needs to be realistic about what they do not know. Above average results are most often achieved by doing ordinary things exceptionally well.

Does the business have a consistent operating history?

In general, the best levels of profits over the long-term are achieved by companies that have been producing the same product or service for a number of years. An investor should never ignore a current business reality because of some vision of future success. Look to buy a business which has shown it can reasonably weather different economic cycles and competitive forces. The best time to buy any business is when profitability has been interrupted for some external short-term reason. This can create a rare one-time opportunity to purchase a sound investment.

Business at an unusually low price, does the business have favourable long-term prospects?

The economic world is divided into a large group of commodity companies and a small group of companies that own the franchise for their product or service. Commodity companies compete solely on price, with no differentiation between suppliers. As well as the traditional oil and gas companies, the commodities group now includes computers, automobiles and airlines. By contrast, a company which own the franchises have a product or service which is needed has no close substitutes and for which an unregulated market exists. Ideally, a business purchaser will want to buy a franchise type of company. These companies have an appreciable margin of safety whereby prices can be raised to offset management mistakes. The only problem is a strong franchise holder soon attracts competitors and substitute products, which in turn leads to the creation of a commodity market around that product or service.

At the age of 25 in 1956, Buffett started an investment partnership. He had seven limited partners who contributed $105,000 and Buffett as general partner put in $100. The limited partners received 6-percent interest per year and 75-percent of the profits generated above this level. Buffett was paid the other 25-percent. Over the next 13 years, this partnership compounded investments at an annual rate of 29.5-percent. In 1965, Buffett closed the partnership and cashed out with a personal stake of $25 million.

"Time is the friend of the wonderful business, the enemy of the mediocre."Warren

"If you thought of yourself as having a card with only twenty punches in a lifetime, and every financial decision used up one punch. You'd resist the temptation to dabble. You'd make more good decisions and you'd make more big decisions." The Snowball: Warren Buffett and the Business of Life.

Warren interested in the company that have durable competitive advantage. Warren separates the world of business into two categories.

- The first, the sickly, are the companies with poor economics. These businesses are in what he calls price-competitive industries that sell commodity type products or services. A price-competitive type of business manufactures or sells a product or service that many other businesses sell and competes for customers solely on the basis of price.

- The second type of business is the healthy. It has terrific business economics working in its favour, made possible by the presence of what Warren calls a durable competitive advantage. A company with a durable competitive advantage typically sells a brand-name product or service that holds a privileged position in the stream of commerce that allows it to price its product or service as if it faces little or no competition, creating a kind of Consumer monopoly. If you want this particular product or service, you have to purchase it from one company and no one else. This gives the company the freedom to raise prices and produce higher earnings. These companies also have the greatest potential for long-term economic growth.

Everybody knows how to hit - but very few really do" Ted Williams

Warren Buffett has long recognised the importance of exercising patience and sticking within your circle of competence when investing. Buffett regularly uses the analogy of the baseball player who only strikes the ball when it's in his or her sweet-spot. Unlike baseball there are no called strikes in investing. An investor can wait for the day a good pitch comes along.

In the recent HBO Documentary 'Becoming Warren Buffett', Buffett notes...

"The trick in investing is just to sit there and watch pitch after pitch go by and wait for the one right in your sweet spot, and if people are yelling, 'Swing, you bum!' ignore them."

That is the power of the brand name. Nike to the running shoe, Coke to the soft drink, Hershey's to the chocolate bar, Wrigley's to gum, McDonald's to the hamburger, Taco Bell to the taco, KFC to fried chicken, and Pizza Hut to pizza. Warren wants to own businesses with high profit margins and high inventory turnover.

Commodity type Business – Airline, Automobile, steel, paper, the consumer make decision to buy the product based on the price factor It is very hard to get rich if you buy such company.

Price-competitive businesses sometimes try to create product distinction by bombarding the buyer with advertising to create a brand name. The idea is to fool buyers into believing that their product is better than the competition's. In some instances, considerable product modifications allow one manufacturer too briefly.

The problem is that no matter what is done to a commodity product or service, if the choice the consumer makes is motivated by price alone, the company that is the low-cost producer will be the winner and the others will end up struggling.

"Warren is fond of saying that when management with an excellent reputation meets a business with a poor reputation, it is usually the business's reputation that remains intact. In other words no matter who is running the show, there is no way to turn an inherently poor business into an excellent one"

Find the company simple to understand have unique product or unique services.

For Warren, the secret is to be fearful when others are greedy and greedy when others are fearful. Bear markets offer the buying opportunity, while bull markets vindicate his bear market investments with big profits.

"There were two thousand auto companies the most important invention, probably, of the first half of the twentieth century. It had an enormous impact on people's lives. If you had seen at the time of the first cars how this country would develop in connection with autos, you would have said, 'This is the place I must be.' But of the two thousand companies, as of a few years ago, only three car companies survived And, at one time or another, all three were selling for less than book value, which is the amount of money that had been put into the companies and left there. So, autos had an enormous impact on America, but in the opposite direction on investors." **The Snowball: Warren Buffett and the Business of Life.**

"Now the other great invention of the first half of the century was the airplane. In this period from 1919 to 1939, there were about two hundred companies. Imagine if you could have seen the future of the airline industry back there at Kitty Hawk. You would have seen a world undreamed of. But assume you had the insight, and you saw all of these people wishing to fly and to visit their relatives or run away from their relatives or whatever you do in an airplane, and you decided this was the place to be. "As of a couple of years ago, there had been zero money made from the aggregate of all stock investments in the airline industry in history. **The Snowball: Warren Buffett and the Business of Life.**

Good jockeys will do well on good horses but not on broken down nags.-warren (Pat win the race)

Manager Matter in context of the moat - The required level of managerial skill inversely related to the quality of the business .

- Bad Business? Better have great Manager (Airline, Automobile).

- Great Business? Genius not needed to run.

Right Business can create wealth mediocre business destroys wealth.

Company Background

Company ticker symbol –

Ticker symbol is an arrangement of characters—usually, letters—representing particular securities listed or traded publicly. When a company issues securities to the public marketplace, it selects an available ticker symbol for its shares. Investors and traders use the ticker symbol to place trade orders.

Name –

An incorporated company name, the most obvious difference between a corporation and other business structures is the ability of corporations to raise large sums of money by selling stock shares to investors. Instead of being cantered on a single person or a small group, ownership of an incorporated business is spread out among stockholders, who have the right to vote on key business decisions.

Corporations are listed on stock exchanges, such as the New York Stock Exchange (NYSE), and anyone can access a wide range of financial and operational data about each company.

Founded Year –

Year of Incorporated Date

Founder & History –

"We study history not to be clever in another time, but to be wise always."

-Marcus Tullius Cicero

Who is the founder and what the history we can understand? Studying history is important because it allows us to understand company past, which in turn allows us to understand company present status. History Helps Us Understand the story of the company, vision to establish.

Company history is a powerful tool that will enable investor to better understand the company's past and to help shape its future. You can't build a framework on which to base your life without understanding how things work in the world. History paints us a detailed picture of how society, technology, and government worked way back when so that we can better understand how it works now. It also helps us determine how to approach the future, as it allows us to learn from our past mistakes. History helps us develop a better understanding of the Company. History makes us better decision makers.

"Those that do not learn history are doomed to repeat it." Those words were first spoken by George Santayana, and they are still very relevant today because of how true they are. History gives us the opportunity to learn from past mistakes. It helps us understand the many reasons why people may behave the way they do. As a result, it helps us become more compassionate as people and more impartial as decision makers

Headquarters –

Place of incorporated

Industries served –

An industry made up of companies that primarily earn revenue through providing products and services.

Current CEO –

A chief executive officer, the highest-ranking person in a company or other institution, ultimately responsible for taking managerial decisions.

Employee –

An employee is a person who is paid to work for an organization.

Revenue –

In accounting, revenue is the income that a business has from its normal business activities, usually from the sale of goods and services to customers.

Profit –

Profit describes the financial benefit realized when revenue generated from a business activity exceeds the expenses, costs, and taxes .

Product Details –

A product is the item offered for sale. A product can be a service or Goods. It can be physical or in virtual or cyber form. Look for product is good or Service. Every product is made at a cost and each is sold at a price. The price that can be charged depends on the market, the quality, the marketing and the segment that is targeted. Each product has a useful life after which it needs replacement, and a life cycle after which it has to be re-invented. In FMCG parlance, a brand can be revamped, re-launched or extended to make it more relevant to the segment and times, often keeping the product almost the same., Good are physical and services are not.

Product wise Revenue % –

Look for Product Segment Report, each product contributes in revenue.

Customer Details –

A customer is an individual or business that purchases another company's goods or services.

Product wise Customer –

Look for Customer in each product segment .

Geographic areas served –

Which all are countries where customers are located. which all country they are operating. Geographic segmentation is when a business divides its market on the basis of geography. There are several ways that a market can be geographically segmented. You can divide your market by geographical areas, such as by city, county, state, region, (like the West Coast), country, or international region, (like Asia). You can also divide the market into rural, suburban, and urban market segments. And, you can segment a market by climate or total population in each area.

It's an effective approach for companies with large national or international markets because different consumers in different regions have different needs, wants, and cultural characteristics that can be specifically targeted.

Revenue Geographic wise % –

The Breakup of revenue Geographical wise.

Main Competitors –

Any person or entity which is a rival against another. In business, a company in the same industry or a similar industry which offers a similar product or service. The primary competitor in the market was spending heavily on marketing and advertising so we decided to match their investment, Competition is not just another business that might take money away from you. It can be another product or service that's being developed and which you ought to be selling or looking to license before somebody else takes it up. Look for Main competitors.

Create Circle of Competence

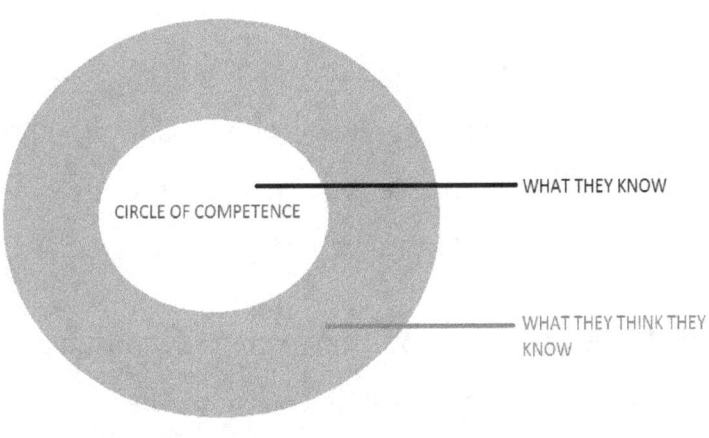

"Everybody's got a different circle of competence. The important thing is not how big the circle is. The important thing is staying inside the circle."

Circle of Competence: What you know and understand. You should always aim to operate within your Circle of Competence, because that is where your efforts will yield the highest reward.

Middle Circle: What you think you know, but actually don't know. This circle is the most dangerous of all. You will make most of your worst mistakes here.

Overconfident people have lost countless fortunes have been lost because they thought they knew what they were doing, but didn't.

Outer Circle: What you don't know, and accept that you don't know. Being aware of what you don't know is just as important as what you do know.

A circle of competence is the subject area which matches a person's skills or expertise. The mental model was developed by Warren Buffett and Charlie Munger to describe limiting one's financial investments in areas where an individual may have limited understanding or experience, concentrating in areas where one has the greatest familiarity, and to emphasize the importance of aligning a subjective assessment of one own's competence with actual competence. Buffett summarized the concept in the motto, "Know your circle of competence, and stick within it. The size of that circle is not very important; knowing its boundaries, however, is vital.

The concept of the Circle of Competence has been used over the years by Warren Buffett as a way to focus investors on only operating in areas they knew best. The concept appears in his **1996 Shareholder Letter:**

What an investor needs are the ability to correctly evaluate selected businesses. Note that word "selected": You don't have to be an expert on every company, or even many. You only have to be able to evaluate companies within your circle of competence. The size of that circle is not very important; knowing its boundaries, however, is vital.

"I'm no genius. I'm smart in spots—but I stay around those spots."

— Tom Watson Sr., Founder of IBM

Buffett describes the circle of competence of one of his business managers, a Russian immigrant with poor English who built the largest furniture store in Nebraska.

Nebraska:

I couldn't have given her $200 million worth of Berkshire Hathaway stock when I bought the business because she doesn't understand stock. She understands cash. She understands furniture. She understands real estate. She doesn't understand stocks, so she doesn't have anything to do with them. If you deal with Mrs. B in what I would call her circle of competence... She is going to buy 5,000 end tables this afternoon (if the price is right). She is going to buy 20 different carpets in odd lots, and everything else like that because she understands carpet. She wouldn't buy 100 shares of General Motors if it was at 50 cents a share.

Charlie's simple prescription:

You have to figure out what your own aptitudes are. If you play games where other people have the aptitudes and you don't, you're going to lose. And that's as close to certain as any prediction that you can make. You have to figure out where you've got an edge. And you've got to play within your own circle of competence.

If you want to be the best tennis player in the world, you may start out trying and soon find out that it's hopeless—that other people blow right by you. However, if you want to become the best plumbing contractor in Bemidji, that is probably doable by two-thirds of you. It takes a will. It takes the intelligence.

But after a while, you'd gradually know all about the plumbing business in Bemidji and master the art. That is an attainable objective, given enough discipline. And people who could never win a chess tournament or stand in center court in a respectable tennis tournament can rise quite high in life by slowly developing a circle of competence—which results partly from what they were born with and partly from what they slowly develop through work.

"If you know nothing about an area and haven't studied the companies and the sector, stay away from it"

"The game of investing is one of making better predictions about the future than other people. How are you going to do that? One way is to limit your tries to areas of competence. If you try to predict the future of everything, you attempt too much." Charles Munger

"You have to know what you know—your circle of competence." Joel Greenblatt

"Don't try to be a jack of all investments. Stick to the field you know best" Bernard Baruch

"Most businesses that I look at are typically rejected within two or three minutes or even less. They are rejected in two or three minutes for one of two reasons – they are either outside the circle of competence or the quick look at the price, market cap and such doesn't make it interesting. They either are things that I don't understand or they are things that don't seem to be cheap by any measure that I would have an interest in."

Mohnish Pabrai

The world's greatest investors said no to shiny, early Microsoft stock because they didn't understand the stuff. Bill Gates even invited Buffett to his summer home in 1991, explaining how personal computers would change everything:

Gates: "You've got to have a computer."

Buffett: "Why?"

Gates: "You can keep track of your stock portfolio."

Buffett: "I only own one stock Berkshire Hathaway."

Gates: "Well, you can do your taxes."

Buffett: "I don't have any income. Berkshire doesn't pay a dividend."

Gates: "It's going to change everything."

Buffett: "Will it change whether people chew gum?"

Gates: "Probably not."

Buffett: "Well, then I'll stick to chewing gum, and you stick to computers."

VALUE INVESTING & BEHAVIOURL FINANCE

Module 3

Financial Performance & Growth

Performance Ratio will indicate that company is good and healthy.

Gross Profit Margin

"What he has found is that companies that have excellent long-term economics working in their favour tend to have consistently higher gross profit margins than those that don't." Consider how Buffett categorizes companies by their gross profit margins:

Gross Profit Margin = Gross Profit / Revenue

Durable advantages: Consistent gross profit margins of 40% or more; think of companies such as Coca-Cola (KO) at 60% and Moody's (MCO) at 73%, Apple at 38%. In India Market companies such as ITC 64%, Nestle India 59%. No competitive advantage: Gross profit margins of less than 20. Examples GM 10%, In India Market companies such as Tata Motors 35%, Hero 30%. Check **the Gross profit Margin Stability for last 5 years.**

Operating Profit Margin

Performance ratio that reflects the percentage of profit a company produces from its operations, prior to subtracting taxes and interest charges, expenses include –Operating Expenses such as SGA, R&D & Depreciation.

Operating Profit Margin = Operating Profit / Revenue

The margin is also known as EBIT (Earnings before Interest and Tax) Margin.

Durable advantages: Consistent operating profit margins of 20% or more; Example Apple 26 %, Indian stock such as ITC 36 %, Nestle India 20 %.

No competitive advantage: Operating profit margins of less than 15%, example GM 4%, Tesla .33 %, Indian stock such as hero 13%.

Check the Operating Profit Margin Stability from last 5 years.

Net Profit Margin

The percentage of profit a company produces from its total revenue

Net Profit Margin = Net Income / Revenue

Durable advantages: Consistent Net Profit Margin of 12% or more; Apple 28%, Indian stock such as ITC 26%, Nestle India 14%.

No competitive advantage: Net Profit Margin of less than 10% example Tesla (2.71%), GM 4.8%, Indian stock such as Hero 10%.

Check the Net Profit Margin Stability for last 5 years.

Return on Equity

The Return on Equity (RoE) is a very important ratio, as it helps the investor assess the return the shareholder earns for every unit of capital invested. RoE measures the entity's ability to generate profits from the shareholders investments. In other words, RoE shows the efficiency of the company in terms of generating profits to its shareholders. Obviously, higher the RoE, the better it is for the shareholders. In fact this is one of the key ratios that help the investor identify investable attributes of the company. To give you a perspective, the average RoE of top Indian companies vary between 14 – 16%. I personally prefer to invest in companies that have a RoE of 18% upwards. This ratio is compared with the other companies in the same industry and is also observed over time.

Also note, if the RoE is high, it means a good amount of cash is being generated by the company; hence the need for external funds is less. Thus a higher ROE indicates a higher level of management performance.

Net Profit / Shareholders Equity

A high ROE could mean a company is more successful in generating profit internally. However, it doesn't fully show the risk associated with that return. A company may rely heavily on debt to generate a higher net profit, thereby boosting the ROE higher.

Good ROE –Coca-Cola 30%, Hershey's 33%, Apple 56%.

Poor ROE –Tesla (15%), GM 16%.

Look for a High ROE Company.

DuPont Ratio

Find out is **company Creating Value to the shareholders**, we look close to DuPont ratio, DuPont analysis was created by Mr. Donaldson Brown in 1920, while he was working at DuPont Corporation. DuPont Analysis is an extended examination of Return on Equity (ROE) of a company which analyses Net Profit Margin, Asset Turnover, and Financial Leverage. DuPont analysis, in its early stage was used for measuring the management efficiency. DuPont Analysis is a tool that may help us to avoid misleading conclusions regarding a company's profitability. This model breaks down the return on equity ratio to explain how companies can increase their return for investors.

Profit Margin: This is a very basic profitability ratio. This is calculated by dividing the net profit by total revenues. This resembles the profit generated after deducting all the expenses. The primary factor remains to maintain healthy profit margins and derive ways to keep growing it by reducing expenses, increasing prices etc, which impacts ROE.

Total Asset Turnover: This ratio depicts the efficiency of the company in using its assets. This is calculated by dividing revenues by average assets. This ratio differs across industries but is useful in comparing firms in the same industry. If the company's asset turnover increases, this positively impacts the ROE of the company.

Financial Leverage: This refers to the debt usage to finance the assets. The companies should strike a balance in the usage of debt. The debt should be used to finance the operations and growth of the company. However, usage of excess leverage to push up the ROE can turn out to be detrimental for the health of the company.

$$ROE = \underbrace{\frac{\text{Net Income}}{\text{Net Sales}}}_{\text{Profit Margin}} \times \underbrace{\frac{\text{Net Sales}}{\text{Total Assets}}}_{\text{Asset Turnover}} \times \underbrace{\frac{\text{Total Assets}}{\text{Total Equity}}}_{\text{Financial Leverage}}$$

The secret of finding great stocks for long term investment is to find stocks that have great ability to preserve investor's capital and create a lot of wealth at the same time.

It gives a broader view of the Return on Equity of the company. It highlights the company's strengths and pinpoints the area where there is a scope for improvement. Say if the shareholders are dissatisfied with lower ROE, the company with the help of DuPont Analysis formula can assess whether the lower ROE is due to low-profit margin, low asset turnover or poor leverage.

Once the management of the company has found the weak area, it may take steps to correct it. The lower ROE may not always be a concern for the company as it may also happen due to normal business operations. For instance, the ROE may come down due to accelerated depreciation in the initial years.

The return on equity (ROE) metric is net income divided by shareholders' equity. The DuPont analysis is still the ROE, just an expanded version. The ROE calculation alone reveals how well a company utilizes capital from shareholders.

With a DuPont analysis, investors and analysts can dig into what drives changes in ROE, or why an ROE is considered high or low. That is, a DuPont analysis can help deduce whether its profitability, use of assets or debt that's driving ROE.

The DuPont Analysis is an excellent method if you want to get an understanding of a company's strengths and weaknesses. Each individual weak financial ratio in the model can be analysed further in order to get more insight in the underlying reason for that weakness. If the calculation of the three components of the DuPont analysis reveals any weaknesses, the Management can take measures, such as improving their cost control, assets management or marketing. The objective of all these measures is to increase the return on equity ratio. The DuPont analysis is useful for making the right investment decisions. It helps in understanding the position of a company in a better way.

Example Apple

APPLE INC ROE 55.92%

21.24%		
PROFIT MARGIN X		55
0.77		260
ASSTES TURNOVER RATIO X		260
3.74		338.52
FINANCIAL LEVERAGE		338.52
		90.49

Example

Let's take a look at A Retailers and B Retailers. Both of these companies operate in the same industry and have the same return on equity ratio of 45 percent. This model can be used to show the strengths and weaknesses of each company. Each company has the following

Ratio	A	B
Profit Margin	30%	15%
Total Asset Turnover	.50	6.0
Financial Leverage	3.0	.50

As you can see, both companies have the same overall ROE, but the companies' operations are completely different.

> **DuPont Analysis**
> 45%=.30x.50x 30
> 45%=.15x.6.0x.50

A is generating sales while maintaining a lower cost of goods as evidenced by its higher profit margin. A is having a difficult time turning over large amounts of sales, using high leverage.

B business, on the other hand, is selling products at a smaller margin, but it is turning over a lot of products. You can see this from its low profit margin and extremely high asset turnover, using low leverage.

Growth in Earnings Per Share

Earnings per share or basic earnings per share are calculated by net income and dividing by the weighted average common shares outstanding. Earnings per share (EPS) ratio measures how many dollars of net income have been earned by each share of common stock during a certain time period. It is computed by dividing net income less preferred dividend by the number of shares of common stock outstanding during the period. It is a popular measure of overall profitability of the company

Earnings per share = Net income/Weighted average number of shares outstanding

Earnings can cause stock prices to rise, and when they do, investors make money. If a company has high earnings per share, it means it has more money available to either reinvest in the business or distribute to stockholders in the form of dividend payments. In either scenario, the investors win Look **for Growth in EPS last 5 -10 years.**

YEAR	EPS	RETURN
2010	2.16	
2011	3.95	45%
2012	6.31	37%
2013	5.68	-11%
2014	6.45	12%
2015	9.22	30%
2016	8.31	-11%
2017	9.21	10%
2018	11.91	23%
2019	11.89	0%
	18.60%	14.99%
CAGR RETURN	18.60%	
AVERAGE RETUN	14.99%	

Growth in Book Value Per Share

The book value per share formula is used to calculate the per share value of a company based on its equity available to common shareholders. The term "book value" is a company's assets minus its liabilities and is sometimes referred to as stockholder's equity, owner's equity, shareholder's equity, or simply equity.

Common stockholder's equity, or owner's equity, can be found on the balance sheet for the company. In the absence of preferred shares, the total stockholder's equity is used. Look for Growth in BVPS last 5 -10 years. Book value per share is just one of the methods for comparison in valuing of a company

BOOK VALUE PER SHARE	TOTAL COMMON STOCKHOLDERS
	NUMBER OF COMMON SHARES

The book value per share may be used by some investors to determine the equity in a company relative to the market value of the company, which is the price of its stock. For example, a company that is currently trading for $20 but has a book value of $10 is selling at twice its equity.

Book value per share is broadly used in relative valuation and usually to compare a firm's market value per share. If a firm's BVPS is higher than its market value per share, then the stock is undervalued, which means that it trades lower than the price that the market determines. **Example APPLE**

YEAR	BVPS	RETURN
2010	7.45	
2011	11.78	37%
2012	16.99	31%
2013	19.6	13%
2014	20.62	5%
2015	22.53	8%
2016	23.71	5%
2017	25.83	8%
2018	24.17	-7%
2019	21.71	-11%
	11.29%	9.91%
CAGR RETURN	11.29%	
AVERAGE RETUN	9.91%	

Return on Capital employed

Return on capital employed (ROCE) is a financial ratio that measures a company's profitability and the efficiency with which its capital is used. In other words, the ratio measures how well a company is generating profits from its capital. The ROCE ratio is considered an important profitability ratio and is used often by investors when screening for suitable investment candidates.

The Formula for ROCE Is

$$ROCE = \frac{EBIT}{Capital\ Employed}$$

where:

EBIT = Earnings before interest and tax

Capital Employed = Total assets − Current liabilities

Operating Income/Return on Capital Employed

Example: Avenue Super Marts Limited

- Capital Employed:

TOTAL ASSETS	6,997.57
CURRENT LIABILITIES	1,212.57
Capital Employed	5,785.00

- Return on Capital Employed:

Capital Employed	5,785.00
EBIT	1,447.64
ROCE	25%

ROCE is used to prove the value the business gains from its assets and liabilities. Companies create value whenever they are able to generate returns on capital above the weighted average cost of capital (WACC). A business which owns lots of land will have a smaller ROCE compared to a business which owns little land but makes the same profit.

It basically can be used to show how much a business is gaining for its assets, or how much it is losing for its liabilities.

Free Cash Flow Return on Capital Employed

A cash basis measure of the profitability of a business that equals free cash flow divided by capital employed.

Free Cash Flow / Capital Employed

It should be above 10%

Example: Apple

Free Cash Flow $58.896 Billion

Capital Employed $232.8 Billion

FCFROCE =25.29 %

Total Liabilities-to-Equity ratio

Companies use a mix of debt and equity to finance their operations. While the cost of debt is typically less than investors' required return on equity, prudent financial management limits the amount of debt a company can support. One measure of the financial health of a company is its ratio of debt to equity.

$$\frac{\text{Total Liabilities}}{\text{Total Equity}}$$

Example Avenue Supermart Ltd	
	INR Cr
Total Liabilities	14183
Total stock holders' equity	55874
Liabilities to Equity Ratio	25%

The Ratio should be less, it indicates that company is have less debts and high equity. Companies with a higher debt to equity ratio are considered riskier to creditors and investors than companies with a lower ratio. Unlike equity financing, debt must be repaid to the lender. Since debt financing also requires debt servicing or regular interest payments, debt can be a far more expensive form of financing than equity financing. Companies leveraging large amounts of debt might not be able to make the payments.

VALUE INVESTING & BEHAVIOURL FINANCE

Module 4

Competitive Advantage

Michael Porter

Porter's Five Forces is a business analysis model that helps to explain why various industries are able to sustain different levels of profitability. The five forces are frequently used to measure competition intensity, attractiveness. Porter's Five Forces Framework is a method for analyzing competition of a business. It draws from industrial organization (IO) economics to derive five forces that determine the competitive intensity and, therefore, the attractiveness (or lack of it) of an industry in terms of its profitability. An "unattractive" industry is one in which the effect of these five forces reduces overall profitability. The most unattractive industry would be one approaching "pure competition", in which available profits for all firms are driven to normal profit levels. The five-force perspective is associated with its originator, Michael E. Porter of Harvard University. This framework was first published in Harvard Business Review in 1979. It has become one of the most popular and highly regarded business strategy tools.

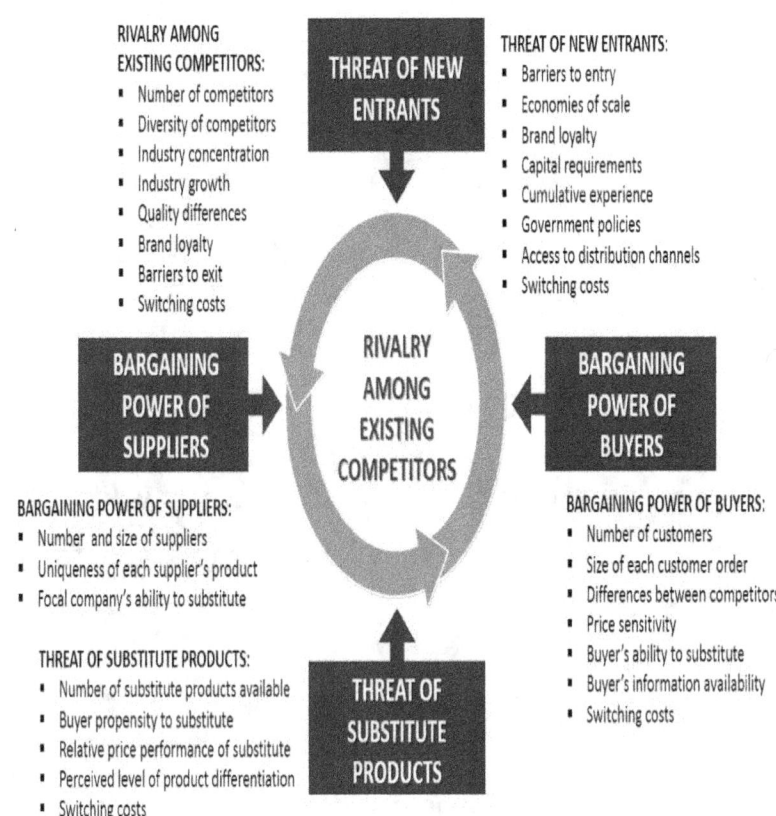

Threat of new entrants

Position can be affected by people's ability to enter your market. A company's power is also affected by the force of new entrants into its market. The less time and money it cost for a competitor to enter a company's market and be an effective competitor.

- Low amount of capital is required to enter a market.

- Existing firms do not possess patents, trademarks or do not have established brand reputation.

- There is no government regulation.

- Customer switching costs are low (it doesn't cost a lot of money for a firm to switch to other industries).

- There is low customer loyalty.

- Products are nearly identical.

- Economies of scale can be easily achieved.

Threat of substitutes

Substitute goods or services that can be used in place of a company's products or services pose a threat. Companies that produce goods or services for which there are no close substitutes will have more power to increase prices and lock in favourable terms. When close substitutes are available, customers will have the option to forgo buying a company's product, and a company's power can be weakened.

- There are many competitors.

- Exit barriers are high.

- Industry of growth is slow or negative.

- Products are not differentiated and can be easily substituted.

- Competitors are of equal size.

- Low customer loyalty.

Bargaining power of customers

How easy it is for buyers to drive your prices down. How many buyers are there, and how big are their orders? How much would it cost them to switch from your products and services to those of a rival? Are your buyers strong enough to dictate terms to you?

- Buying in large quantities or control many access points to the final customer.

- Only few buyers exist.

- Switching costs to another supplier are low.

- There are many substitutes.

- Buyers are price sensitive.

Bargaining power of suppliers

This is determined by how easy it is for your suppliers to increase their prices. How many potential suppliers do you have? How unique is the product or service that they provide, and how expensive would it be to switch from one supplier to another.

- There are few suppliers but many buyers.

- Few substitute raw materials exist.

- Suppliers hold scarce resources.

- Cost of switching raw materials is especially high.

Competitive Rivalry

This looks at the number and strength of your competitors. How many rivals do you have? Who are they, and how does the quality of their products and services compare with yours.

- Number of competitors.

- Cost of leaving an industry.

- Industry growth rate and size.

- Product differentiation.

- Competitors' size.

- Customer loyalty.

- Threat of horizontal integration.

Example –Apple Inc

Bargaining power of customers: LOW

- Company enjoys the pricing power.

Bargaining power of suppliers: LOW

- Only couple of suppliers are very specific might result in low bargaining power.

Threat of substitutes: High

- The markets for the Company's products and services are highly competitive and the Company is confronted by aggressive competition in all areas of its business. These markets are characterized by frequent product introductions and rapid technological advances that have substantially increased the capabilities and use of mobile communication and media devices, personal computers and other digital electronic devices. The Company's competitors that sell mobile devices and personal computers based on other operating systems have aggressively cut prices and lowered their product margins to gain or maintain market share. The Company's financial condition and operating results can be adversely affected by these and other industry-wide downward pressures on gross margins. Principal competitive factors important to the Company include price, product features (including security features), relative price and performance, product quality and reliability, design innovation, a strong third-party software and accessories ecosystem, marketing and distribution capability, service and support and corporate reputation.

Threat of new entrants: Low

- The Company currently holds rights to patents and copyrights relating to certain aspects of its hardware devices, accessories, software and services. The Company has registered or has applied for trademarks and service marks in the

U.S. and a number of foreign countries. Although the Company believes the ownership of such patents, copyrights, trademarks and service marks is an important factor in its business and that its success does depend in part on such ownership, the Company relies primarily on the innovative skills, technical competence and marketing abilities of its personnel.

Competitive Rivalry: HIGH

- Company has huge competition in product wise.

Example Amazon

Competitive rivalry or competition High

- Directly competes against giants like Wal-Mart, which has a significant and expanding e-commerce website. Amazon also experiences the strong force of substitutes because of their high availability. For instance, Wal-Mart's physical or brick-and-mortar stores are substitutes to Amazon's online retail service. Other brick-and-mortar bookstores and smaller retailers also compete against Amazon.

Bargaining power of buyers or customers High

- In terms of the ability of customers to find alternatives to the company's online retail service. In relation, the low switching costs make it easy for consumers to transfer from Amazon to other firms, such as Walmart. Also, the high availability of substitutes further empowers consumers to shift from one retailer to another.

Bargaining power of suppliers Low

- Changes in prices of equipment from a small number of large suppliers could directly impact the company's online retail operational costs. However, the moderate forward integration limits suppliers' actual effect on Amazon.

Threat of substitutes or substitution High

- The low switching costs show that customers can easily transfer from the company to other retailers. For example, consumers can easily decide to buy from Walmart stores or other retail establishments instead of buying from Amazon.com Inc. The high availability of substitutes and the low costs of their product offerings further increase the influence of substitutes against the company.

Threat of new entrants or new entry Low

- It would take years and billions of dollars to create a strong brand that directly competes with the Amazon brand. In addition, the company benefits from high economies of scale that makes its e-commerce business strong. As such, new entrants need to achieve similarly high economies of scale to compete against the company.

Understanding Moats

"The most important thing to me is figuring out how big a moat there is around the business. What I love, of course, is a big castle and a big moat with piranhas and crocodiles."

Warren E. Buffett

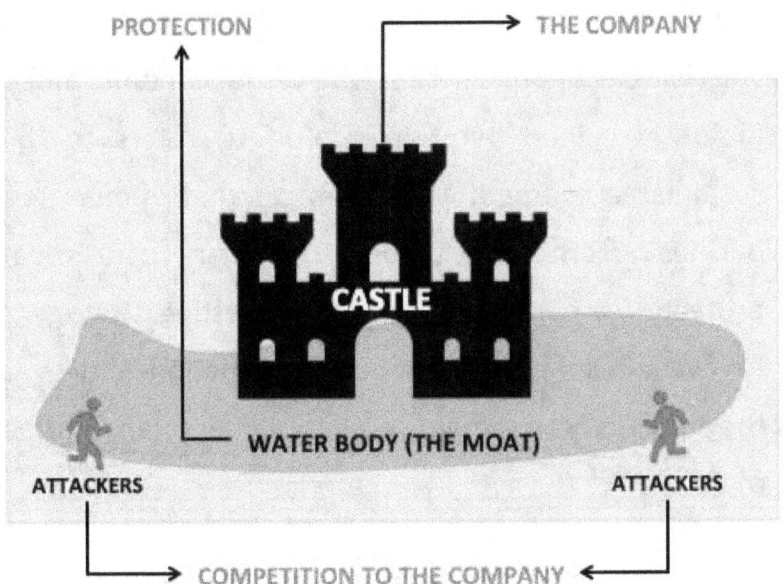

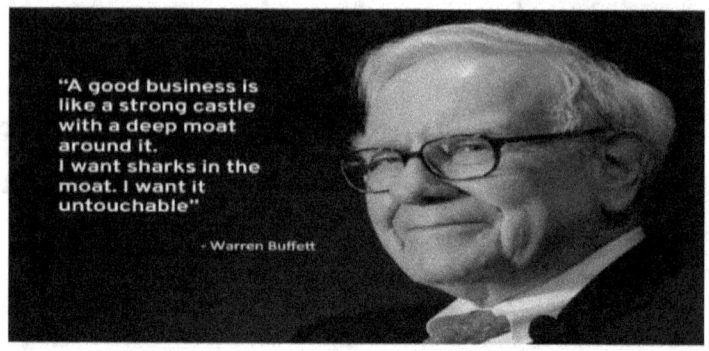

When Warren Buffett stated "It's far better to buy a wonderful company at a fair price than a fair company at a wonderful price," he was talking about companies with wide economic moats. The term Economic moat, famously coined by Warren Buffett, refers to the sustainable competitive advantages that immunize a business from competitors – similar to a moat protecting a castle. Mr. Buffett's investing strategy is to invest in companies with strong economic moats as they are likely to remain successful over a long period of time.

A competitive advantage is essentially any factor that allows a company to provide a good or service that is similar to those offered by its competitors and, at the same time, outperforms those competitors in profits. A good example of a competitive advantage would be a low-cost advantage, such as cheap access to raw materials. Very successful investors such as Buffett have been adept at finding companies with solid economic moats but relatively low share prices.

One of the basic tenets of modern economics, however, is that, given time, competition will erode any competitive advantages enjoyed by a firm. This effect occurs because once a firm establishes competitive advantages, its superior operations generate boosted profits for itself, thus providing a strong incentive for competing firms to duplicate the methods of the leading firm or find even better operating methods.

Quite simply, an economic moat is a long-term competitive advantage that allows a company to earn oversized profits over time. The term was coined by one of our favorite investors of all time, Warren Buffet, who realized that companies that reward investors over the long term have a durable competitive advantage. Assessing that advantage involves understanding what kind of defense, or competitive barrier, the company has been able to build for itself in its industry.

Moats are important from an investment perspective because any time a company develops a useful product or service; it isn't long before other firms try to capitalize on that opportunity by producing a similar--if not better--product. Basic economic theory says that in a perfectly competitive market, rivals will eventually eat up any excess profits earned by a successful business. In other words, competition makes it difficult for most firms to generate strong growth and profits over an extended period of time since any advantage is always at risk of imitation.

The strength and sustainability of a company's economic moat will determine whether the firm will be able to prevent a competitor from taking business away or eroding its earnings. In our view, companies with wide economic moats are best positioned to keep competitors at bay over the long term, but we also use the terms "narrow" and "none" to describe a company's moat. We don't often talk about the depth of a moat, yet it's a good way of thinking about how much money a company can make with its advantage.

1. Evaluate the firm's historical profitability. Has the firm been able to generate a solid return on its assets and on shareholder equity? This is probably the most important component to identifying whether or not a company has a moat. While much about assessing a moat is qualitative, the bedrock of analyzing a company still relies on solid financial metrics.

2. Assuming that the firm has solid returns on its capital and is consistently profitable, try to identify the source of those profits. Is the source an advantage that only this company has, or is it one that other company can easily imitate? The harder it is for a rival to imitate an advantage, the more likely the company has a barrier in its industry and a source of economic profit.

3. Estimate how long the company will be able to keep competitors at bay. We refer to this time period as the company's competitive advantage period, and it can be as short as several months or as long as several decades. The longer the competitive advantage period, the wider the economic moat.

4. Think about the industry's competitive structure. Does it have many profitable firms or is it hypercompetitive with only a few companies scrounging for the last dollar? Highly competitive industries will likely offer less attractive profit growth over the long haul.

Investing in companies with wide economic moats can give the investor considerable benefits.

Identifying moats enables the investor to invest in companies that are going to be around for the long run, but they would be able to sustain their profitability.

Identifying if a business has a Moat or not helps in avoiding overpaying for a stock which might be going through a short-term advantage which cannot be defended by any sustainable competitive advantage. Once the short-term advantage is lost, the profitability could be impacted and the market would then value the business very differently.

Companies with moats are more likely to recover from temporary setbacks. Investing in economic moats means that the odds of permanently losing capital are reduced significantly.

Just the identification of an Economic Moat is not sufficient to ensure a solid investment. Once a moat has been identified, it must be analyzed further to understand its sources. The health of the moat needs to be verified. That is, is it a moat that is a narrowing one? Or are there any possible threats to its advantages in the future? For example, a patent or process that is easily replicable. The longevity of the moat is an important consideration. The more sustainable the moat, the stronger it is considered to be.

A competitive advantage is essentially any factor that allows a company to provide a good or service that is similar to those offered by its competitors and, at the same time, outperforms those competitors in profits. A good example of a competitive advantage would be a low-cost advantage, such as cheap access to raw materials. Very successful investors such as Buffett have been adept at finding companies with solid economic moats but relatively low share prices.

Creating an Economic Moat

- **Intangible assets**

- **Customer Switching Costs**

- **Cost advantage**

- **Efficient Scale**

- **Network Effect**

Intangible Assets

Another type of economic moat can be created through a firm's intangible assets, which includes items such as patents, brand recognition, government licenses and others. Strong brand name recognition allows these types of companies to charge a premium for their products over other competitors' goods, which boosts profits.

- Includes brands, patents, and regulatory licenses.

- Brand increases the customer's willingness to pay.

- Patents protect pricing power legally barring competition.

- Government regulations hinder competitors from market.

Example Company is Coca cola, Unilever, and Johnson & Johnson.

Customer Switching Costs

When a company is able to establish itself in an industry, suppliers and customers can be subject to high switching costs should they choose to do business with a new competitor. Competitors have a very difficult time taking market share away from the industry leader because of these cumbersome switching costs.

- Time is money.

- The cost of switching exceeds the expected value of the benefit.

- Razor and blade model entrench repeat consumables customers.

- Price not the only determinant.

Example Company is Oracle, Apple.

Cost advantage

A cost advantage that competitors cannot replicate can be a very effective economic moat. Companies with significant cost advantages can undercut the prices of any competitor that attempts to move into their industry, either forcing the competitor to leave the industry or at least impeding its growth. Companies with sustainable cost advantages can maintain a very large market share of their industry by squeezing out any new competitors who try to move in

- Sustainably lower costs than competitors
- Irreplaceable process advantages
- Superior location
- Hard-to-amass scale
- Access to a unique asset

Example Company is Amazon.

Efficient Scale

This is when more units of a good or service can be produced on a larger scale with lower input costs. This reduces overhead costs in areas such as financing, advertising, production, etc. Large companies that compete in a given industry tend to dominate the core market share of that industry.

- Dynamic in which a market of limited size is effectively served by few companies.

- Newcomers discouraged from entering because returns in the market fall below the cost of capital.

Example Company is Walmart.

Network Effect

A network effect is the effect described in economics and business that an additional user of goods or services has on the value of that product to others. When a network effect is present, the value of a product or service increases according to the number of others using it.

The value of a particular good or service increases for both new and existing users as more customers use that good or service.

With each additional node, the number of potential connections grows exponentially.

Example Master Card, Facebook, Microsoft office.

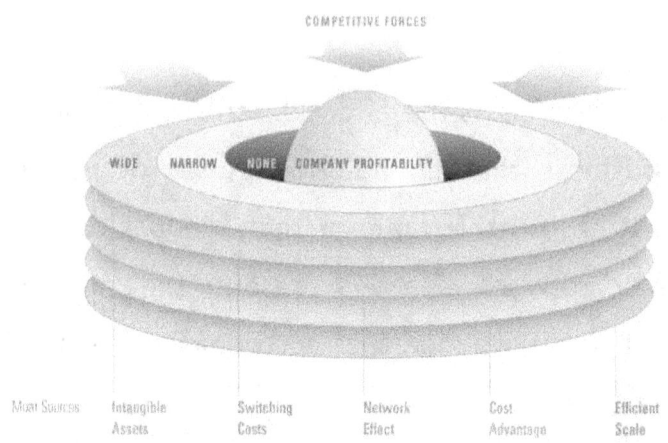

Moat Sources: Intangible Assets | Switching Costs | Network Effect | Cost Advantage | Efficient Scale

Intangible Assets | Switching Costs | Network Effect | Cost Advantage | Efficient Scale

Wide | Narrow | None

Sources of Economic Moats

- Network Effect

- Cost Advantage

- Intangible Assets

- Switching Costs

- New! Efficient Scale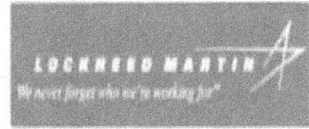

VALUE INVESTING & BEHAVIOURL FINANCE

Module 5

SWOT Analysis

Albert S. Humphrey

SWOT analysis (or SWOT matrix) is a strategic planning technique used to help a person or organization identify strengths, weaknesses, opportunities, and threats related to business competition or project planning. It is designed for use in the preliminary stages of decision-making processes and can be used as a tool for evaluation of the strategic position of a city or organization. It is intended to specify the objectives of the business venture or project and identify the internal and external factors that are favourable and unfavourable to achieving those objectives. Users of a SWOT analysis often ask and answer questions to generate meaningful information for each category to make the tool useful and identify their competitive advantage.

SWOT has been described as the tried-and-true tool of strategic analysis but has also been criticized for its limitations. Strengths and weakness are frequently internally-related, while opportunities and threats commonly focus on the external environment. The name is an acronym for the four parameters the technique examines:

SWOT stands for Strengths, Weaknesses, Opportunities, and Threats, and so a SWOT Analysis is a technique for assessing these four aspects of your business.

SWOT ANALYSIS

	Helpful to achieving the objective	Harmful to achieving the objective
Internal origin (attributes of the organization)	Strengths	Weaknesses
External origin (attributes of the environment)	Opportunities	Threats

Strengths

Strengths are things that your organization does particularly well, or in a way that distinguishes you from your competitors. Think about the advantages your organization has over other organizations. These might be the motivation of your staff, access to certain materials, or a strong set of manufacturing processes.

Strengths are internal, positive attributes of your company. These are things that are within your control.

- What business processes are successful?

- What assets do you have in your team, such as knowledge, education, network, skills, and reputation?

- What physical assets do you have, such as customers, equipment, technology, cash, and patents?

- What competitive advantages do you have over your competition?

Weaknesses

Weaknesses, like strengths, are inherent features of your organization, so focus on your people, resources, systems, and procedures. Think about what you could improve, and the sorts of practices you should avoid.

Weaknesses are negative factors that detract from your strengths. These are things that you might need to improve on to be competitive.

- Are there things that your business needs to be competitive?

- What business processes need improvement?

- Are there tangible assets that your company needs, such as money or equipment?

- Are there gaps on your team?

- Is your location ideal for your success?

Opportunities

Think about good opportunities you can spot immediately. These don't need to be game-changers: even small advantages can increase your organization's competitiveness. What interesting market trends are you aware of, large or small, which could have an impact? Opportunities are external factors in your business environment that are likely to contribute to your success.

- Is your market growing and are there trends that will encourage people to buy more of what you are selling?

- Are there upcoming events that your company may be able to take advantage of to grow the business?

- Are there upcoming changes to regulations that might impact your company positively?

- If your business is up and running, do customers think highly of you?

Threats

Think about the obstacles you face in getting your product to market and selling. You may notice that quality standards or specifications for your products are changing, and that you'll need to change those products if you're to stay in the lead. Evolving technology is an ever-present threat, as well as an opportunity!

Threats are external factors that you have no control over. You may want to consider putting in place contingency plans for dealing them if they occur.

- Do you have potential competitors who may enter your market?

- Will suppliers always be able to supply the raw materials you need at the prices you need?

- Could future developments in technology change how you do business?

- Is consumer behaviour changing in a way that could negatively impact your business?

Strengths	**Weaknesses**
Characteristics of a business which give it advantages over its competitors	Characteristics of a business which make it disadvantageous relative to competitors
Opportunities	**Threats**
Elements in a company's external environment that allow it to formulate and implement strategies to increase profitability	Elements in the external environment that could endanger the integrity and profitability of the business

Example- Apple Inc

Strengths

Strong and extensive U.S. distribution channels Apple's strength in the U.S. is its extensive distribution channels. Apple is well-known for employing multiple channels to deliver its products to customers. The company uses direct distribution channels such as its online stores, direct sales force, and most notably, retail stores. Few of its rivals have their own physical retail stores and none have such a vast network of them.

Apple is a vertically integrated company that manages four separate businesses as one. The company has a hardware business, a software business and it is also a service-provider and a retailer as well – all integrated into one entity.

This means that the company's brand is the most reputable and recognizable in the world. Apple's leading position in the Smartphone marketplace, its excellent advertising and marketing capabilities, and the wide ecosystem of its products has led to a brand awareness that cannot be matched by any other technology company in the world.

Sound financial performance with one of the strongest cash flows.

The company's growth, net income, cash reserves and low debt provide it with enough resources to invest in acquisitions, R&D, marketing and other cash draining activities without significantly threatening its financial situation.

Weaknesses

This makes Apple very vulnerable to changes in the smartphone market. Apple's smartphones are targeting wealthier consumers and its biggest sales come from developed regions where the smartphones' markets are already saturated. Overdependence on iPhone sales.

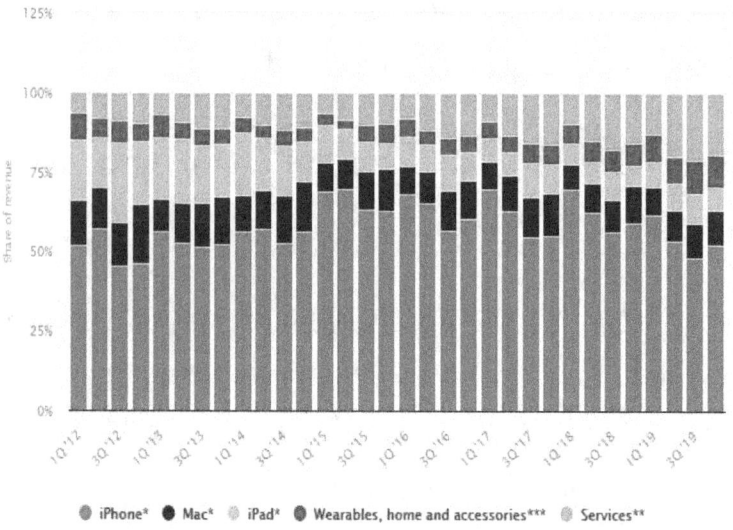

Opportunities

Health-related wearable gadgets could be introduced to the market, smart watch called Apple Watch. This is the first company's step into the wearable gadgets market, which is expected to grow by 35% rate on average each year until 2019. Smart watches are not the only opportunity for Apple in the wearable gadgets market. There is a trend toward health-related wearable gadgets. The company could introduce its own range of wearable health gadgets, which for example could monitor calorie intake, sugar and hydration levels, heart rate and blood pressure, as well as potentially diagnosing many illnesses or even infusing drugs through the skin.

The mobile payments market provides an opportunity that would greatly benefit Apple in terms of additional revenue, strengthened ecosystem and better user experience.

Threats

Intensifying competition puts pressure on Apple's market share, revenue and profits, Apple has always faced strong competition from Microsoft, IBM, HP and Dell in the personal computing sector and since the launch of the iPhone and iPad, that competition has increased significantly. Now Apple's main rivals are Google and Samsung, both well-funded and experienced competitors which work together to provide the best possible offerings to compete with Apple's devices. Apple with its high-end but overpriced devices is likely to lose the battle for emerging markets to cheaper Android devices. Strong

U.S. dollar Currency exchange rates affect every multinational company, including Apple. The company earns over 65% of its revenue outside of the U.S.

Example -Microsoft

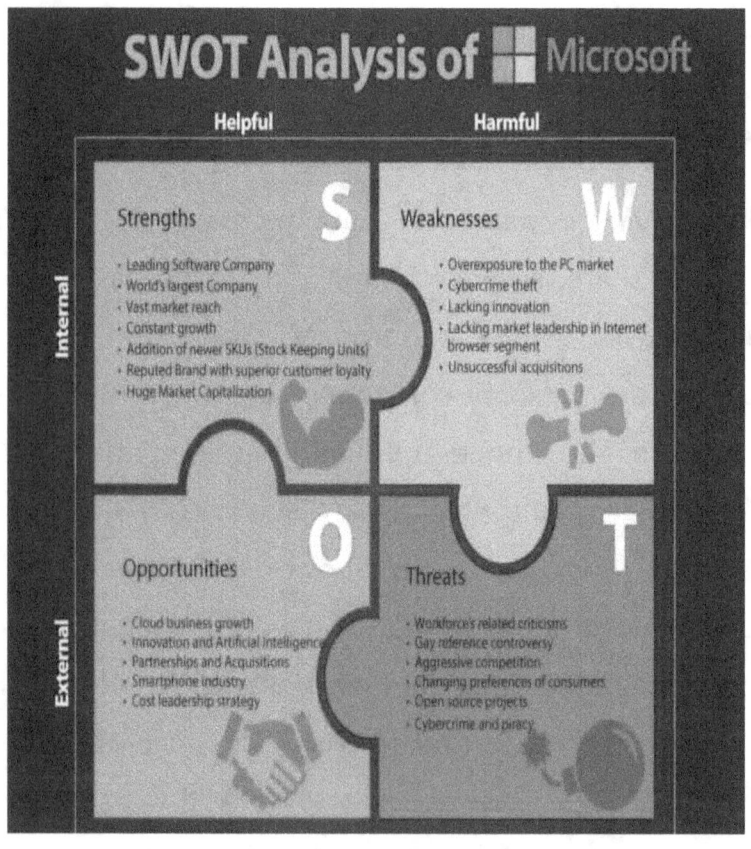

Example Wal-Mart Inc.

Walmart SWOT

Strengths

- Global organizational size.
- Global supply chain.
- High efficiency of supply chain.

Weaknesses

- Thin profit margins.
- Easily copied business model.
- Competitive disadvantage against high-end specialty sellers.

Opportunities

- Expansion in developing countries.
- Improvement in human resource practices to develop competitiveness in the labour market Improvement in quality standards.

Threats

- Healthy lifestyle trend.
- Aggressive competition.
- Online retailers of various sizes.

BCG Matrix

Bruce Doolin Henderson

BCGmatrix, Boston matrix, Boston Consulting Group analysis, portfolio diagram is a chart that was created by Bruce D. Henderson for the Boston Consulting Group in 1970 to help corporations to analyze their business units, that is, their product lines. This helps the company allocate resources and is used as an analytical tool in brand marketing, product management, strategic management, and portfolio analysis. Some analysis of market performance by firms using its principles.

The Boston Consulting group's product portfolio matrix (BCG matrix) is designed to help with long-term strategic planning, to help a business consider growth opportunities by reviewing its portfolio of products to decide where to invest, to discontinue or develop products. It's also known as the Growth/Share Matrix.

Relative market share - One of the dimensions used to evaluate business portfolio is relative market share. Higher corporate's market share results in higher cash returns. This is because a firm that produces more, benefits from higher economies of scale and experience curve, which results in higher profits. Nonetheless, it is worth to note that some firms may experience the same benefits with lower production outputs and lower market share.

Market growth rate - High market growth rate means higher earnings and sometimes profits but it also consumes lots of cash, which is used as investment to stimulate further growth. Therefore, business units that operate in rapid growth industries are cash users and are worth investing in only when they are expected to grow or maintain market share in the future.The Matrix is divided into 4 quadrants based on an analysis of market growth and relative market share, as shown in the diagram below.

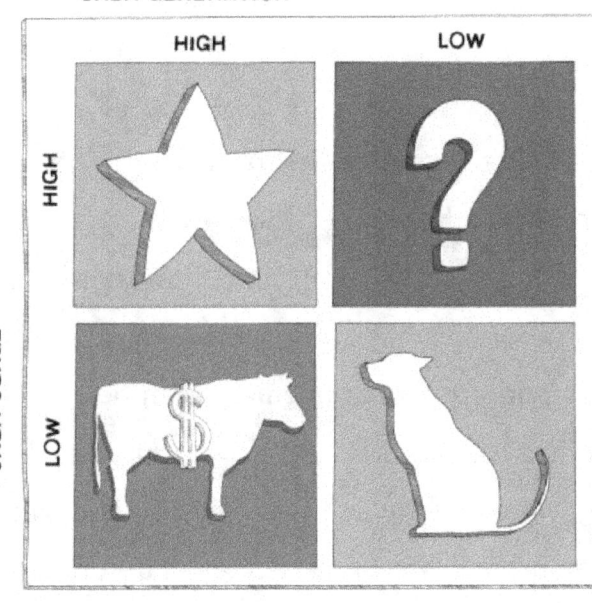

The BCG Matrix is actually based on the product lifecycle as you can see in the diagram below.

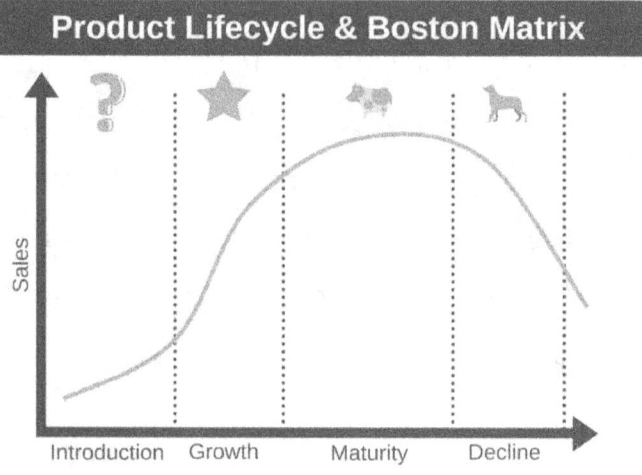

Dogs

These are products with low growth or market share. Dogs hold low market share compared to competitors and operate in a slowly growing market. In general, they are not worth investing in because they generate low or negative cash returns. But this is not always the truth. Some dogs may be profitable for long period of time; they may provide synergies for other brands or simple act as a defence to counter competitor's moves. Therefore, it is always important to perform deeper analysis of each brand to make sure they are not worth investing in or have to be divested.

Question Marks

Products in high growth markets with low market share. Question marks are the brands that require much closer consideration. They hold low market share in fast growing markets consuming large amount of cash and incurring losses. It has potential to gain market share and become a star, which would later become cash cow. Question marks do not always succeed and even after large amount of investments they struggle to gain market share and eventually become dogs. Therefore, they require very close consideration to decide if they are worth investing in or not.

Stars

Products in high growth markets with high market share. Stars operate in high growth industries and maintain high market share. Stars are both cash generators and cash users. They are the primary units in which the company should invest its money, because stars are expected to become cash cows and generate positive cash flows. Yet, not all stars become cash flows. This is especially true in rapidly changing industries, where new innovative products can soon be outcompeted by new technological advancements, so a star instead of becoming a cash cow, becomes a dog.

Cash Cows

Products in low growth markets with high market share. Cash cows are the most profitable brands and should be "milked" to provide as much cash as possible. The cash gained from "cows" should be invested into stars to support their further growth. According to growth-share matrix, corporate should not invest into cash cows to induce growth but only to support them so they can maintain their current market share. Again, this is not always the truth. Cash cows are usually large corporations that are capable of innovating new products or processes, which may become new stars. If there would be no support for cash cows, they would not be capable of such innovations.

Each of the four quadrants represents a specific combination of relative market share, and growth:

Low Growth, High Share. Companies should milk these "cash cows" for cash to reinvest.

High Growth, High Share. Companies should significantly invest in these "stars" as they have high future potential.

High Growth, Low Share. Companies should invest in or discard these "question marks," depending on their chances of becoming stars.

Low Share, Low Growth. Companies should liquidate, divest, or reposition these "pets."

Example Apple Inc

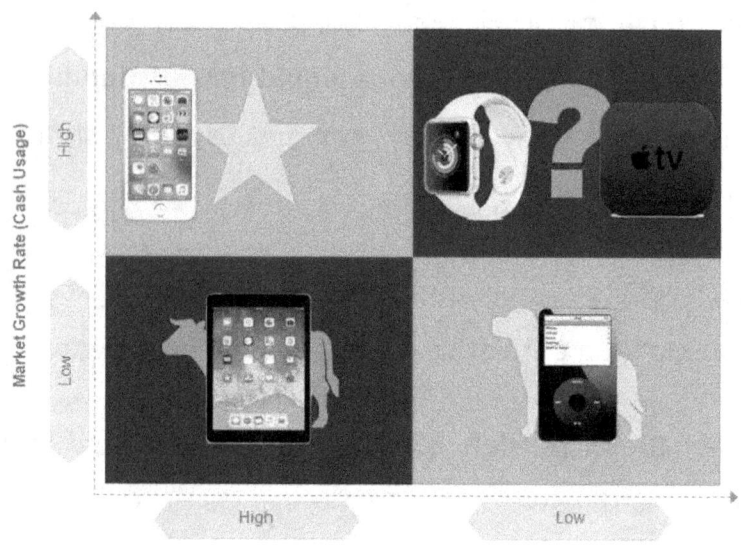

CASH COWS:

There are two products of Apple that fall under the Cash Cow category of BCG Matrix of Apple, the first being Apple iTunes and the second being Apple MacBook and iMac's.

Over the year's iTunes, MacBook and iMac's have attained the position of being a Cash Cow for the company. The company has carved a niche for itself and has its own base of loyalists who prefer Apple products only.

But since the computing industry is slowly becoming portable and mobile, the need to have laptops and desktops are also decreasing, hence we can add Apple iMac and MacBooks in Dogs category as well.

STARS:

The business units that represent the star of an organization also share the feature of having a high market share, but what makes them different from cash cows are that their respective industry can still expand further.

For Apple, their iPhones are undoubtedly are the Stars for them. With every new launch of Apple iPhone, the company manages to set new sales records.

Known for its design and technology prowess, Apple iPhones have its own set of loyalists thanks to which it easily manages to stride off the competition available in the market. Apple iPad and Apple Smartwatch are also regarded as the Stars for the company and are currently in the transition to become the Cash Cows for the company.

QUESTION MARK:

Apple TV makes a bit of money, but it's not reaching its true potential.

If Apple can solve a few ecosystem problems, they could really own the TV space. There are tons of rumours of an Apple TV product that might just maybe dominate like the iPod/iPhone/i Pad.

DOGS:

Dogs are those products that were perceived to have the potential to grow but however failed to create magic due to the slow market growth.

Failure to deliver the expected results makes the product a source of loss for the organization, propelling the management to withdraw future investment in the venture. Since the product is not expected to bring in any significant capital, future investment is seen as wastage of company resources, which could be invested in a Question mark or Star category instead.

Apple iPods were considered the next big thing when they were introduced in the market but eventually failed to create a significant impact due to high competition and low customer demand.

Example Microsoft

Example ITC

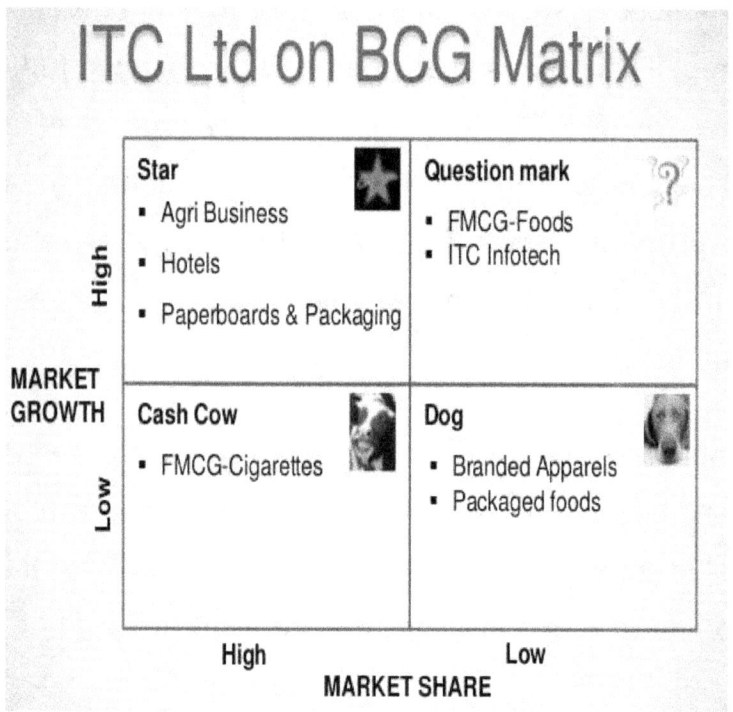

VALUE INVESTING & BEHAVIOURL FINANCE

Module 6
Management Integrity and Rationality

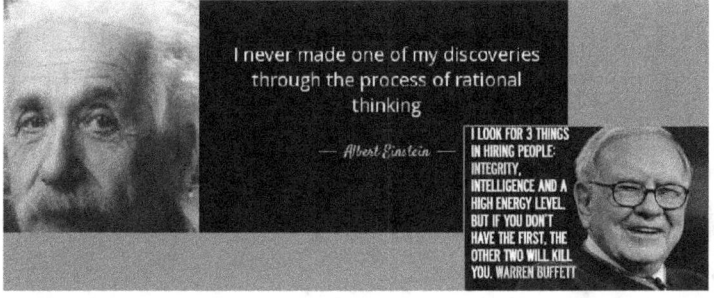

Good managers need a variety of managerial skill in order to successfully manage a large group of people, specifically the skill of management integrity. Additionally, managers must utilize the resources of their employer to an optimal degree. The importance of integrity for managers is one of the key managerial skills. A manager's subordinates must trust, and even look up to, their supervisor. Without managerial integrity, the employees may not perform at their highest levels. Indeed, motivating the employees can be a make-or-break mark for a successful manager. Business managers have to utilize the physical, emotional, mental, and intellectual talents of their employees in order to successfully run business operations.

In fact, ethics has *everything* to do with management. Rarely do the character flaws of a lone actor fully explain corporate misconduct. More typically, unethical business practice involves the tacit, if not explicit, cooperation of others and reflects the values, attitudes, beliefs, language, and behavioral patterns that define an organization's operating culture. Ethics, then, is as much an organizational as a personal issue. Managers who fail to provide proper leadership and to institute systems that facilitate ethical conduct share responsibility with those who conceive, execute, and knowingly benefit from corporate misdeeds.

- Inquiries of management and those charged with governance regarding fraud controls past fraud cases, and how management dealt with them.

- Open communication with employees regarding management's practices and ethical behaviour.

- Evaluating the company's code of ethics and the message it delivers to employees about management's tolerance of unethical behaviour.

- Understanding the extent of management's involvement in related-party transactions.

- Conducting background checks on managers.

- Checking if management had any financial statements restatements history.

- Asking the same question in multiple forms to determine whether a manager tends to hide information or falsify facts.

Example Geico

Berkshire has beaten the market by investing in companies with strong leadership. Over the last 40 years, the company has returned 20 percent annually, double the S&P 500's return over the same time span .Buffett put this management strategy into play at insurer Geico.

Buffett first bought stock in the insurance company when he 20 years old, eventually owned 41 percent of the company. In his 1986 letter to shareholders, Buffett credited Geico Chairman Bill Snyder with keeping operating costs low. Buffett called that the "most important ingredient" to the company's success.

"In sum, Geico is an exceptional business run by exceptional managers," he wrote. "We are fortunate to be associated with them."

Buffett agreed to purchase the rest of Geico for $2.3 billion in 1995. Gaining control of the growing company and its strong management was worth the high cost, he wrote in his letter that year. Buffett highlighted Tony Nicely, who rose from his position at the company as a clerk to become the chairman of the company.

In 1995, Buffett praised nicely, who is still the chairman, for his intelligence, energy and focus, saying "If we're lucky, he'll stay another 34 years."

Compensation & Ownership

Financial compensation refers to the act of providing a person with money or other things of economic value in exchange.

Check the A proxy statement is a statement required of a firm when soliciting shareholder votes. This statement is filed in advance of the annual meeting. The firm needs to file a proxy statement, otherwise known as a Form DEF 14A, with the U.S. Securities and

Exchange Commission, for Indian company check Annual Report.

CEO stands for Chief Executive Officer. The word "officer" infers the person is an officer of a corporation, which is owned by stockholders. If the CEO owns even one share of stock in the company that employees him, he is an owner.

Example Apple Inc

Profile - Tim Cook Chief Executive Officer.

Executive Compensation Tables

Summary Compensation Table—2018, 2017, and 2016

The following table, footnotes, and related narrative show information regarding the total compensation of each named executive officer for 2018, 2017, and 2016, except in the case of Ms. Adams and Mr. Williams, who were not named executive officers in 2017 or 2016.

Name and Principal Position (a)	Year (b)	Salary(1) ($)(c)	Bonus ($)(d)	Stock Awards(2) ($)(e)	Non-Equity Incentive Plan Compensation(3) ($)(f)	All Other Compensation ($)(g)	Total ($)(h)
Tim Cook	2018	3,000,000	—	—	12,000,000	682,219(4)	15,682,219
Chief Executive Officer	2017	3,057,692	—	—	9,327,000	440,374	12,825,066
	2016	3,000,000	—	—	5,370,000	377,719	8,747,719

Compensation = $ 15682219

Compensation with Revenue = Compensation/Revenue = .006%

(It should be less than 1 %)

Ownership=847,969

Security Ownership of Certain Beneficial Owners and Management

The following table shows information as of January 2, 2020 (the "Table Date"), unless otherwise indicated, regarding the beneficial ownership of Apple's common stock by: (i) each person known to Apple to beneficially own more than 5% of the outstanding shares of Apple's common stock based solely on Apple's review of filings with the SEC pursuant to Section 13(d) or 13(g) of the Exchange Act; (ii) each director and nominee; (iii) each named executive officer listed in the table entitled "Summary Compensation Table – 2019, 2018, and 2017" under the section entitled "Executive Compensation"; and (iv) all current directors and executive officers as a group. As of the Table Date, 4,384,027,000 shares of Apple's common stock were issued and outstanding. Unless otherwise indicated, all persons named as beneficial owners of Apple's common stock have sole voting power and sole investment power with respect to the shares indicated as beneficially owned.

Name of Beneficial Owner	Shares of Common Stock Beneficially Owned[1]	Percent of Common Stock Outstanding
The Vanguard Group	338,533,988[2]	7.72%
BlackRock, Inc.	296,598,349[3]	6.77%
Berkshire Hathaway Inc. / Warren E. Buffett	255,300,329[4]	5.82%
Kate Adams	22,639[5]	*
Angela Ahrendts	30,848	*
James Bell	7,716[6]	*
Tim Cook	847,969[7]	*
Al Gore	115,014[8]	*

Share Repurchases

Look in Annual Report

Share repurchase (or stock buyback or share buyback) is the re-acquisition by a company of its own stock. It represents a more flexible way (relative to dividends) of returning money to shareholders.

In most countries, a corporation can repurchase its own stock by distributing cash to existing shareholders in exchange for a fraction of the company's outstanding equity; that is, cash is exchanged for a reduction in the number of shares outstanding.

Companies typically have two uses for profits. Firstly, some part of profits can be distributed to shareholders in the form of dividends or stock repurchases. The remainder of profits are retained earnings, kept inside the company and used for investing in the future of the company, if profitable ventures for reinvestment of retained earnings can be identified. However, sometimes companies may find that some or all of their retained earnings cannot be reinvested to produce acceptable returns.

Share repurchases are an alternative to dividends. When a company repurchases its own shares, it reduces the number of shares held by the public. The reduction of the float, or publicly traded shares, means that even if profits remain the same, the earnings per share increase. Repurchasing shares when a company's share price is undervalued benefits non-selling shareholders (frequently insiders) and extracts value from shareholders who sell. There is strong evidence that companies are able to profitably repurchase shares when the company is widely held by retail investors who are unsophisticated (e.g., small investors) and more likely to sell their shares to the company when those shares are undervalued. By contrast, when the company is held primarily by insiders and institutional investors, who are more sophisticated, it is harder for companies to profitably repurchase shares. Companies can also more readily repurchase shares at a profit when the stock is liquidly traded and the companies' activity is less likely to move the share price.

A transaction whereby a company buys back its own shares from the marketplace. A company might buy back its shares because management considers them undervalued. The company buys shares directly from the market or offers its shareholders the option of tendering their shares directly to the company at a fixed price.

Because a share repurchase reduces the number of shares outstanding, it increases earnings per share (EPS). A higher EPS elevates the market value of the remaining shares.

Successful companies generate profits, and one thing that many publicly traded businesses do with some of that cash is make share repurchases. A share repurchase is simply when a company chooses to buy back some of its own stock, typically on the open market, with the help of a financial institution as an intermediary. And while they are a more subtle way of sharing a company's economic prosperity with its stakeholders than a dividend increase, buybacks can profit investors too.

When a board of directors authorizes a share repurchase program, it typically states either the number of shares the company is interested in buying back or a dollar amount it will spend on its stock buyback. The net impact of a share repurchase is to reduce the number of outstanding shares, which boosts the much-watched earnings-per-share metric even if overall net income remains flat. Given that stock valuations are often viewed through the lenses of EPS and the related price-earnings ratio, higher EPS justifies (and can lead to) a rising share price.

A difference in tax treatment makes share repurchases more attractive to many shareholders. With dividends, all investors who hold shares in taxable accounts have to pay taxes on their dividend income. By contrast, with share repurchases, only those shareholders who choose to sell their shares pay tax on their capital gains.

Example Apple Capital Return Program

The following table presents the Company's dividends, dividend equivalents, share repurchases and net share settlement activity from the start of the capital return program in August 2012 through September 24, 2016 (in millions):

	Dividends and Dividend Equivalents Paid	Accelerated Share Repurchases	Open Market Share Repurchases	Taxes Related to Settlement of Equity Awards	Total
2016	$ 12,150	$ 12,000	$ 17,000	$ 1,570	$ 42,720
2015	11,561	6,000	30,026	1,499	49,086
2014	11,126	21,000	24,000	1,158	57,284
2013	10,564	13,950	9,000	1,082	34,596
2012	2,488	—	—	56	2,544
Total	$ 47,889	$ 52,950	$ 80,026	$ 5,365	$ 186,230

The Company expects to execute its capital return program by the end of March 2018 by paying dividends and dividend equivalents, repurchasing shares and remitting withheld taxes related to net share settlement of restricted stock units. The Company plans to continue to access the domestic and international debt markets to assist in funding its capital return program.

Dividends

When a corporation earns a profit or surplus, it is able to pay a proportion of the profit as a dividend to shareholders. Any amount not distributed is taken to be re-invested in the business (called retained earnings) the dividend received by a shareholder is income of the shareholder and may be subject to income tax (see dividend tax). The tax treatment of this income varies considerably between jurisdictions. The corporation does not receive a tax deduction for the dividends it pays.

In financial history of the world, the Dutch East India Company (VOC) was the first recorded (public) company ever to pay regular dividends. The VOC paid annual dividends worth around 18 percent of the value of the shares for almost 200 years of existence (1602–1800).

Dividend refers to a reward, cash or otherwise, that a company gives to its shareholders. Dividends can be issued in various forms, such as cash payment, stocks or any other form. A company's dividend is decided by its board of directors and it requires the shareholders' approval. However, it is not obligatory for a company to pay dividend. Dividend is usually a part of the profit that the company shares with its shareholders.

Example: Apple

The Company paid a total of $12.6 billion in dividends during 2017 and 2016, respectively, and expects to pay quarterly dividends of $0.63 per common share each quarter, subject to declaration by the Board of Directors. The Company also plans to increase its dividend on an annual basis, subject to declaration by the Board of Directors.

Example: JOHNSON & JOHNSON

The Company increased its dividend in 2016 for the 54th consecutive year. Cash dividends paid were $3.15 per share in 2016 compared with dividends of $2.95 per share in 2015, and $2.76 per share in 2014.

Inside Purchase

Look in Proxy statement for US company, for Indian Company Annual Report Beneficial owners of more than 2% of a class of equity securities of a publicly traded company to file a report with the SEC. Look for the inside Purchase.

Example: Apple Inc

Security Ownership of Certain Beneficial Owners and Management

The following table shows information as of January 2, 2020 (the "Table Date"), unless otherwise indicated, regarding the beneficial ownership of Apple's common stock by: (i) each person known to Apple to beneficially own more than 5% of the outstanding shares of Apple's common stock based solely on Apple's review of filings with the SEC pursuant to Section 13(d) or 13(g) of the Exchange Act; (ii) each director and nominee; (iii) each named executive officer listed in the table entitled "Summary Compensation Table – 2019, 2018, and 2017" under the section entitled "Executive Compensation"; and (iv) all current directors and executive officers as a group. As of the Table Date, 4,384,027,000 shares of Apple's common stock were issued and outstanding. Unless otherwise indicated, all persons named as beneficial owners of Apple's common stock have sole voting power and sole investment power with respect to the shares indicated as beneficially owned.

Name of Beneficial Owner	Shares of Common Stock Beneficially Owned[1]	Percent of Common Stock Outstanding
The Vanguard Group	338,533,988[2]	7.72%
BlackRock, Inc.	296,598,349[3]	6.77%
Berkshire Hathaway Inc. / Warren E. Buffett	255,300,329[4]	5.82%

Related Party transactions

In business, a related party transaction is a transaction that takes place between two parties who hold a pre-existing connection prior to the transaction. An example is how a dominant shareholder may benefit from making one of their company's trade to the other at advantageous prices. A related-party transaction is a deal or arrangement between two parties who are joined by a pre-existing business relationship or common interest. In the United States, securities industry regulatory agencies help to ensure that related-party transactions are conflict-free and do not affect shareholders value or the corporation's profits negatively.

Example: JOHNSON & JOHNSON

Transactions with Related Persons for 2019

A sister-in-law of Paulus Stoffels, Vice Chairman of the Executive Committee and Chief Scientific Officer, is a Senior Manager at Janssen Pharmaceutica NV, a wholly owned subsidiary of the Company, and earned $166,309 in total compensation in 2019 (using an exchange rate of 1.1144USD/1 EUR), including base salary, any annual incentive bonus, the value of any long-term incentive award granted in 2019, and any other compensation. She also participates in the general welfare and benefit plans of Janssen Pharmaceutica NV. Her compensation was established in accordance with Janssen Pharmaceutica NV's employment and compensation practices applicable to employees with equivalent qualifications and responsibilities and holding similar positions. Dr. Stoffels does not have a material interest in his sister-in-law's employment, nor does he share a household with her.

A sister of Joseph J. Wolk, Executive Vice President, Chief Financial Officer, is a Talent Mobility Advisory Services Leader at Johnson & Johnson Services, Inc., a wholly owned subsidiary of the Company, and earned $200,723 in total compensation in 2019, including base salary, any annual incentive bonus, the value of any long-term incentive award granted in 2019, and any other compensation. She also participates in the general welfare and benefit plans of Johnson & Johnson Services, Inc. Her compensation was established in accordance with Johnson & Johnson Services, Inc.'s employment and compensation practices applicable to employees with equivalent qualifications and responsibilities and holding similar positions. Mr. Wolk does not have a material interest in his sister's employment, nor does he share a household with her.

VALUE INVESTING & BEHAVIOURL FINANCE

Module 7
Margin of Safety

Margin of safety is a principle of investing in which an investor only purchases securities when their market price is significantly below their intrinsic value. In other words, when the market price of a security is significantly below your estimation of its intrinsic value, the difference is the margin of safety. Because investors may set a margin of safety in accordance with their own risk preferences, buying securities when this difference is present allows an investment to be made with minimal downside risk.

"You don't drive a truck that weighs 9,000 pounds across the bridge that says 'limit 10,000 pounds' because you can't be that sure about it."

You value it at $10, and current market price is exactly $ 10. Buying makes complete sense to you. Stop there. Wait for the price to fall to let's say $ 7 whatever and then BUY. This gives you a 30% margin of safety.

Buy a stock at discount to its intrinsic value. In other words buy at bargain. The margin of safety for an investment is the difference between the real or fundamental value and the price you pay. The goal of the value investor is pay less (hopefully, much less) than the real value.

The greater the margin the more leeway you have for negative conditions before you lose money. On the other hand, if conditions are as you expected or better, profits are exponentially higher the greater the original margin.

Here is an example of exponentially higher returns. You have estimated the fundamental value of a stock to be $50 and you purchase it with a 20% margin of safety ($40). If your stock reaches your fundamental value you have a 25% return ($50 divided by $40). However if you purchased the stock with a 50% margin ($25), you have a 100% profit ($50 divided by $25).

The function of the margin of safety is, in essence, that of rendering unnecessary an accurate estimate of the future. If the margin is a large one, then it is enough to assume that future earnings will not fall far below those of the past in order for an investor to feel sufficiently protected against the vicissitudes of time.

Have a true investment, there must be present a true margin of safety. And a true margin of safety is one that can be demonstrated by figures, by persuasive reasoning, and by reference to a body of actual experience.

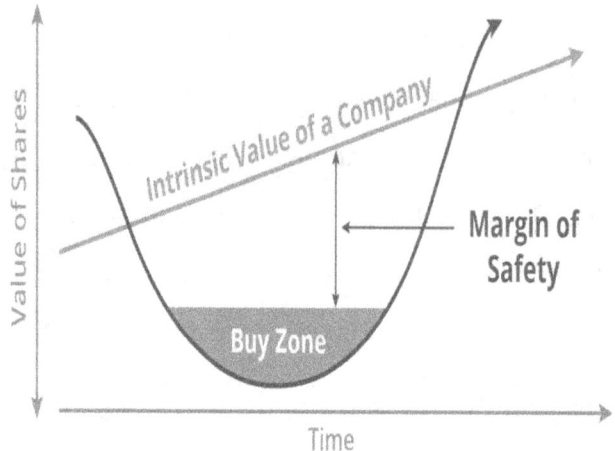

In his speech – The Super investors of Graham-and-Dodd – Warren Buffett defined margin of safety as "buying 1 dollar for 50 cents."

Buffett said…

You also have to have the knowledge to enable you to make a very general estimate about the value of the underlying businesses. But you do not cut it close. That is what Ben Graham meant by having a margin of safety. You don't try and buy businesses worth $83 million for $80 million. You leave yourself an enormous margin.

When you make an investment the laws of probability apply since the decisions involves risk, uncertainty and ignorance. Many people make the mistake of assuming that buying a quality business ensures safety.

As Howard Marks puts it best in his book The Most Important Thing…

…most investors think quality, as opposed to price, is the determinant of whether something's risky. But high quality assets can be risky, and low quality assets can be safe. It's just a matter of the price paid for them….Elevated popular opinion, then, isn't just the source of low return potential, but also of high risk. Similarly, just because the price of share of stock in a company is beaten down from formerly high levels does not make it "safe" to buy.

The margin of safety concept is about making it likely that you have the odds significantly in your favour by trying to find a substantial cushion in terms of the odds.

Value investor Seth Klarman in his classic book Margin of Safety writes...

Because investing is as much an art as a science, investors need a margin of safety. A margin of safety is achieved when securities are purchased at prices sufficiently below underlying value to allow for human error, bad luck, or extreme volatility in a complex, unpredictable, and rapidly changing world.

According to Graham, 'The margin of safety is always dependent on the price paid. For any security, it will be large at one price, small at some higher price, nonexistent at some still higher price.'

Warren Buffett describes margin of safety concept using this example – *"When you build a bridge, you insist it can carry 30,000 pounds, but you only drive 10,000- pound trucks across it and that same principle works in investing."*

To better deal with inevitable mistakes we all make as human beings, you should have built into the process a "margin" of sufficient size which ensures that even if mistakes happen the outcome will be "adequate", as Ben Graham describes.

To quote Munger

In engineering, people have a big margin of safety. But in the financial world, people don't give a damn about safety. They let it balloon and balloon and balloon. It's aided by false accounting.

Valuation

EV to EBITDA

What is EV?

EV stands for Enterprise Value and is the numerator in the EV/EBITDA ratio. A firm's EV is equal to its equity value (or market capitalization) plus its debt (or financial commitments) less any cash (debt less cash is referred to as net debt). The simple formula for enterprise value is:

EV = Market Capitalization + Market Value of Debt – Cash and Equivalents

EBITDA stands for Earnings before Interest, Taxes, Depreciation, and Amortization and is a metric used to evaluate a company's operating performance.

> *Good Valuation is below 8.*

Enterprise value/EBITDA (more commonly referred to by the acronym EV/EBITDA) is a popular valuation multiple used in the finance industry to measure the value of a company. It is the most widely used valuation multiple based on enterprise value.

This popular metric is used as a valuation tool to compare the value of a company, debt included, to the company's cash earnings less non-cash expenses. It's ideal for analysts and investors looking to compare companies within the same industry.

Typically, EV/EBITDA values below 8 are seen as healthy. However, the comparison of relative values among companies within the same industry is the best way for investors to determine companies with the healthiest EV/EBITDA within a specific sector.

$$Enterprise\ Multiple = \frac{EV}{EBITDA}$$

Example: Apple Inc

Apple Inc., current EV/EBITDA calculation, comparison to benchmarks

Selected Financial Data (US$ in millions)

Enterprise value (EV)	1,138,289
Earnings before interest, tax, depreciation and amortization (EBITDA)	81,860

Valuation Ratio

EV/EBITDA	13.91

Benchmarks

EV/EBITDA, Competitors[1]

Advanced Micro Devices Inc.	79.28
Applied Materials Inc.	12.12
Broadcom Inc.	13.18
Cisco Systems Inc.	9.43
Intel Corp.	7.16
Micron Technology Inc.	3.86

Example: Facebook

Facebook Inc., current EV/EBITDA calculation, comparison to benchmarks

Selected Financial Data (US$ in millions)

Enterprise value (EV)	411,211
Earnings before interest, tax, depreciation and amortization (EBITDA)	30,573

Valuation Ratio

EV/EBITDA	13.45

Benchmarks

EV/EBITDA, Competitors[1]

Adobe Inc.	37.92
Alphabet Inc.	13.27
International Business Machines Corp.	8.77
Intuit Inc.	29.42
Microsoft Corp.	19.39

Example: Amazon

Amazon.com Inc., current EV/EBITDA calculation, comparison to benchmarks

Selected Financial Data (US$ in millions)

Enterprise value (EV)	970,142
Earnings before interest, tax, depreciation and amortization (EBITDA)	37,351

Valuation Ratio

EV/EBITDA	25.97

Benchmarks

EV/EBITDA, Competitors[1]

Costco Wholesale Corp.	19.79
Home Depot Inc.	13.13
Lowe's Cos. Inc.	10.96
Target Corp.	7.85
TJX Cos. Inc.	11.25

MCAP/FCF

Price to free cash flow is an equity valuation metric used to compare a company's per-share market price to its per-share amount of free cash flow (FCF). This metric is very similar to the valuation metric of price to cash flow but is considered a more exact measure, owing to the fact that it uses free cash flow, which subtracts capital expenditures (CAPEX) from a company's total operating cash flow, thereby reflecting the actual cash flow available to fund non-asset-related growth. Companies use this metric when they need to expand their asset bases either in order to grow their businesses or simply to maintain acceptable levels of free cash flow.

The price-to-free cash flow ratio is not the same as the price-to-cash flow ratio. The difference between the two is that the former subtracts capital expenditures from cash flow, thereby leaving cash flow that is available to drive non-asset-related growth.

> Good Valuation is below 8.

$$\text{Price to FCF} = \frac{\text{Market Capitalization}}{\text{Free Cash Flow}}$$

Example Apple Inc

Apple's share price is $258.44. Apple's, Free Cash per Share for the trailing twelve months (TTM) ended in Dec. 2019 was $14.13. Hence, Apple's Price-to-Free-Cash-Flow Ratio for today is 18.29.

MCAP/BV

The Market to Book ratio (also called the Price to Book ratio), is a financial valuation metric used to evaluate a company's current market value relative to its book value. The market value is the current stock price of all outstanding shares (i.e. the price that the market believes the company is worth). The book value is the amount that would be left if the company liquidated all of its assets and repaid all of its liabilities. The book value equals the net assets of the company and comes from the balance sheet. In other words, the ratio is used to compare a business's net assets that are available in relation to the sales price of its stock.

> *Good Valuation is below 2.*

A low ratio (less than 2) could indicate that the stock is and a higher ratio (greater than 2) could mean the stock is overvalued.

Market to Book Ratio Formula

$$\text{Market to Book Value} = \frac{\text{Market Capitalization}}{\text{Book Value}}$$

$$\text{Market to Book Value} = \frac{\text{Price Per Share}}{\text{Book Value Per Share}}$$

Example Apple

Apple's share price is $258.44. Apple's Book Value per Share for the quarter that ended in Dec. 2019 was $20.42. Hence, Apple's P/B Ratio of today is 12.65.

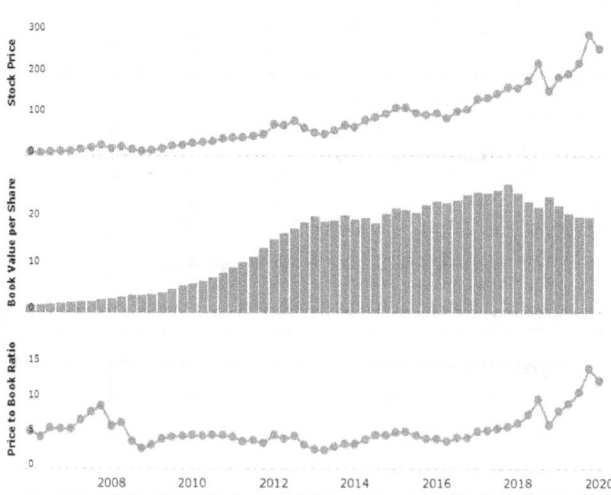

Example Amazon

Amazon share price is USD 1955.49. Amazon Book Value per Share for the fiscal year that ended in Dec. 2019 was USD 124.62. Hence, Amazon P/B Ratio of today is 15.69.

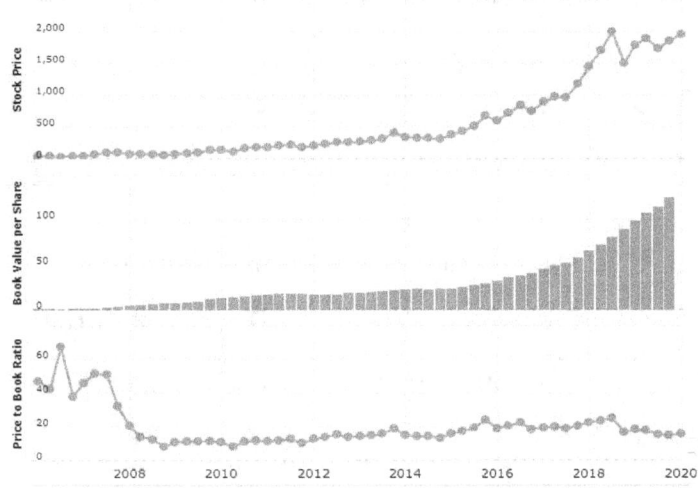

PEG Ratio

The PEG ratio uses the basic format of the P/E ratio for a numerator and then divides by the potential growth for EPS, which you'll have to estimate. The two ratios may seem to be very similar but the PEG ratio is able to take into account future earnings growth. A very generally rule of thumb is that *any*

PEG ratio below 1.0 is considered to be a good value.

The 'PEG ratio' (price/earnings to growth ratio) is a valuation metric for determining the relative trade-off between the price of a stock, the earnings generated per share (EPS), and the company's expected growth

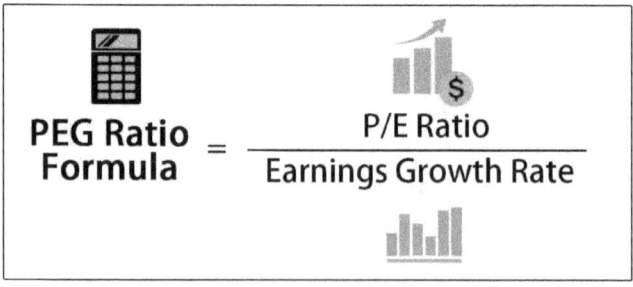

In general, the P/E ratio is higher for a company with a higher growth rate. Thus, using just the P/E ratio would make high-growth companies appear overvalued relative to others. It is assumed that by dividing the P/E ratio by the earnings growth rate, the resulting ratio is better for comparing companies with different growth rates.

The PEG ratio is considered to be a convenient approximation. It was originally developed by Mario Farina who wrote about it in his 1969 Book, A Beginner's Guide to Successful Investing in the Stock Market. It was later popularized by Peter Lynch, who wrote in his 1989 book One Up on Wall Street that "The P/E ratio of any company that's fairly priced will equal its growth rate. The growth rate is expressed as a percent value, and should use real growth only, to correct for inflation. A lower ratio is "better" (cheaper) and a higher ratio is "worse" (expensive) Example Company 1

$$PEG\ ratio\ (company\ 1) = \frac{18\ times\ earnings}{12\%} = 1.5$$

The P/E ratio is a key component of the PEG ratio. You can calculate the P/E by taking a stock's current share price and dividing it by its earnings per share (EPS). This number allows you to compare the relative value of a stock against other stocks, as well as determine if the market has priced a stock higher or lower in relation to its earnings.

Example Apple inc

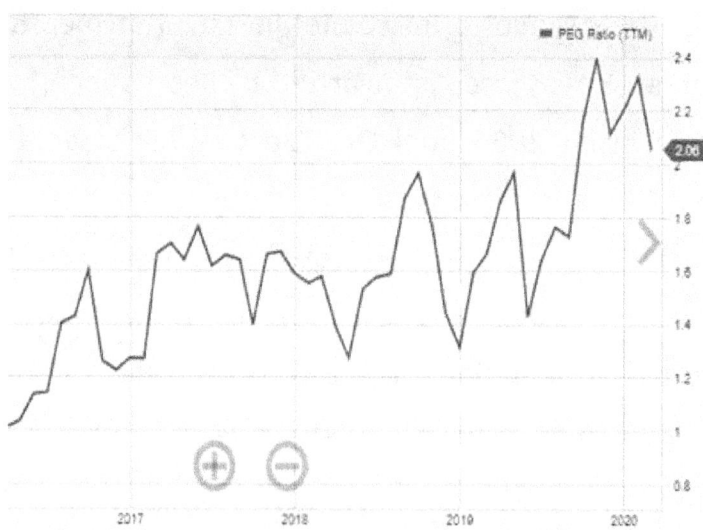

Example Amazon

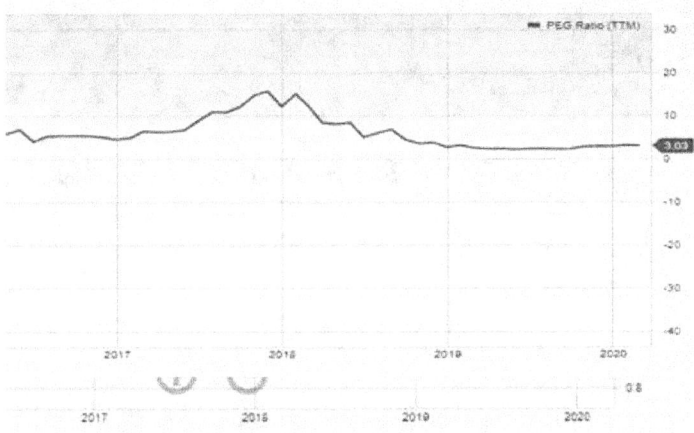

Example Johnson & Johnson

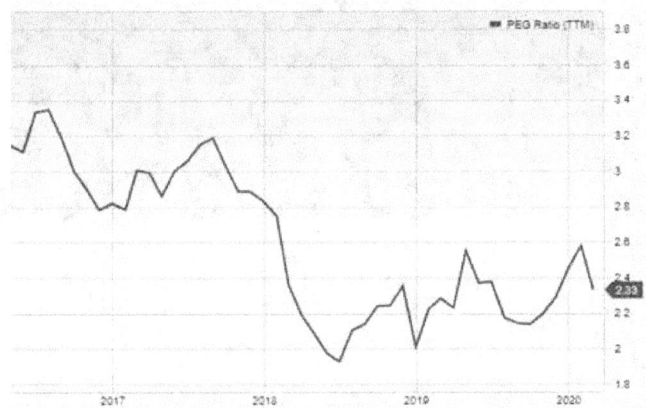

VALUE INVESTING & BEHAVIOURL FINANCE

Module 8

Behavioral Finance

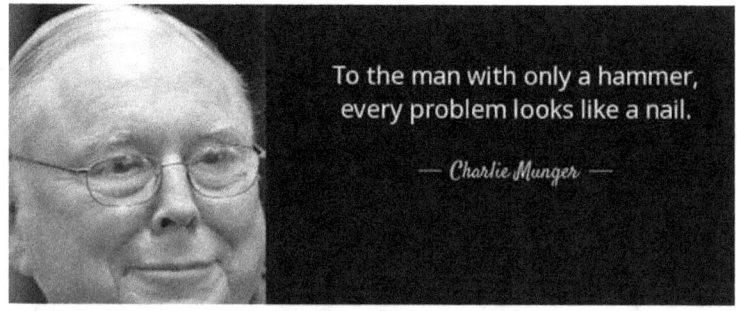

If all you have is a Hammer, everything looks like a nail!

Those who have been around long enough would clearly understand the sparsity of ethical models in leadership. There are too many conflicts on where is the line drawn between a good model and a misguided conviction?

The infamous Charlie Munger of Berkshire Hathaway answers it all. What are the models? Well, the first rule is that you've got to have multiple models because if you have one or two that you're using, the nature of human psychology is such that you'll torture reality so that it fits your models, or at least you'll think it does.

It's like the old saying, "To the man with only a hammer, every problem looks like a nail." And of course, that's the way the chiropractor goes about practicing medicine. But that's an utterly disastrous way to think and an ideally harmful way to operate in the world. So you've got to have multiple models.

The models have to come from multiple disciplines because all the wisdom of the world cannot be found in one little academic department. That's why poetry professors, by and large, are so unwise in a worldly sense. They don't have enough models in their heads.

So, you've got to have models across a fair array of disciplines - says Munger.

Behavioral finance is study of how human interprets and act on information to make informed investment decisions.

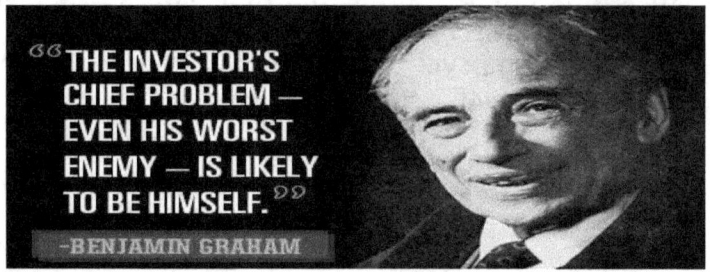

Behavioral finance is the study of the influence of psychology on the behaviour of investors or financial analysts. It also includes the subsequent effects on the markets. It focuses on the fact that investors are not always rational, have limits to their self-control, and are influenced by their own biases.

Traditional Finance focuses on how individuals should behave Behavioral Finance recognizes that the way the information is presented to investors can affect how they make decisions and it can lead to emotional and cognitive biases.

Standard Finance	Behavioral Finance
Standard Finance believes in existence of Rational Markets and Rational investors	Behavioral Finance believe in existence of irrational markets and irrational Investors
It helps in building a rational portfolio	Behavioral finance helps in building an optimal portfolio
Standard Finance theories rest on the assumptions that oversimplify the real market conditions	Explanations of behavioral finance are in light with the real problems associated with human psychology
Standard Finance explains how investor "should" behave	Behavioral Finance explains how "does" behave
Standard Finance assumptions believe in idealized financial	Behavioral finance assumptions believe in observed financial

Behavioral finance can be analyzed from a variety of perspectives. Stock market returns are one area of finance where psychological behaviours are often assumed to influence market outcomes and returns but there are also many different angles for observation. The purpose of classification of behavioral finance is to help understand why people make certain financial choices and how those choices can affect markets. Within behavioral finance, it is assumed that financial participants are not perfectly rational and self-controlled but rather psychologically influential.

One of the key aspects of behavioral finance studies is the influence of biases. Biases can occur for a variety of reasons. Understanding and classifying different types of behavioral finance biases can be very important when narrowing in on the study or analysis of industry or sector outcomes and results.

Behavioral finance is the study of psychology and sociology on the behaviour of the financial practitioners and their effect on the security market. It helps to understand why people buy or sell stock without doing fundamental analysis and behave irrationally in investment decisions.

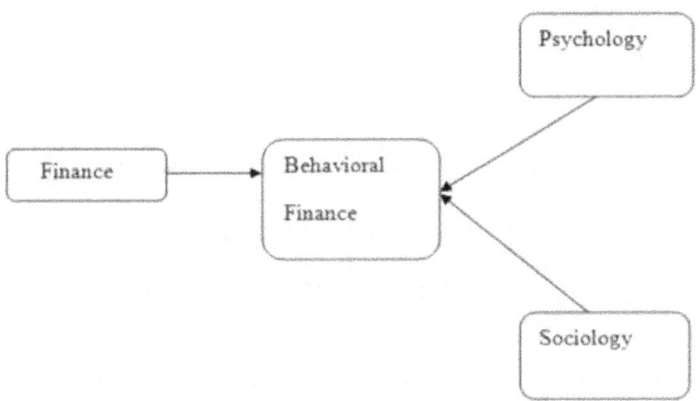

- Traditional finance theories dismissed the idea that people's own psychology can work against them in making good investment decisions.

- Behavioral finance argues that some financial phenomena can plausibly be understood using models in which some agents are not fully rational.

This means that they behave rationally so they earn returns for the money they put in stock markets. To become successful in the stock market it is essential for investors to have rational behaviour patterns.

Rational behaviour is also required to overcome tendencies

- Modern theory of investors' decision-making suggests that investors do not act rationally at every time while making an investment decision.

- They deal with several cognitive and psychological errors. These errors are called behavioral biases and are exists in many ways.

Eugene Fama - "The market price at any time instant reflects all available information in the market".

The importance of psychology in investing is elegantly summarized by the great value investor Warren Buffett in a short paragraph below.

In his 2011 interview, Warren Buffett was quizzed on the qualities that made him a great investor. Was it his intelligence or the discipline that he had?

To which, he replied, "The good news I can tell you is that to be a great investor you don't have to have a terrific IQ. If you've got 160 IQ, sell 30 points to somebody else because you won't need it in investing. What you do need is the right temperament. You need to be able to detach yourself from the views of others or the opinions of others."

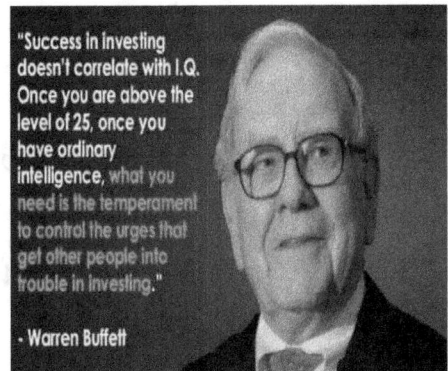

"Know yourself and the enemy and you will emerge triumphant even for a hundred battles".

You are able to exploit the weaknesses in the financial market by remaining calm and composed.

Benoit Mandelbrot claimed the efficient markets theory was first proposed by the French mathematician Louis Bachelier in 1900 in his PhD thesis "The Theory of Speculation" describing how prices of commodities and stocks varied in markets

The efficient markets theory was not popular until the 1960s when the advent of computers made it possible to compare calculations and prices of hundreds of stocks more quickly and effortlessly. In 1945, F.A. Hayek argued that markets were the most effective way of aggregating the pieces of information dispersed among individuals within a society. Given the ability to profit from private information, self-interested traders are motivated to acquire and act on their private information. In doing so, traders contribute to more and more efficient market prices. In the competitive limit, market prices reflect all available information and prices can only move in response to news. Thus there is a very close link between EMH and the random walk hypothesis.

Efficient Market Hypothesis (EMH)

The efficient market hypothesis (EMH), alternatively known as the efficient market theory, is a hypothesis that states that share prices reflect all information and consistent alpha generation is impossible. According to the EMH, stocks always trade at their fair value on exchanges, making it impossible for investors to purchase undervalued stocks or sell stocks for inflated prices. Therefore, it should be impossible to outperform the overall market through expert stock selection or market timing, and the only way an investor can obtain higher returns is by purchasing riskier investments.

The efficient market hypothesis (EMH) or theory states that share prices reflect all information.

- The EMH hypothesizes that stocks trade at their fair market value on exchanges.

- Proponents of EMH posit those investors benefit from investing in a low-cost, passive portfolio.

- Opponents of EMH believe that it is possible to beat the market and that stocks can deviate from their fair market values.

There are three forms of EMH: weak, semi-strong, and strong. Here's what each says about the market.

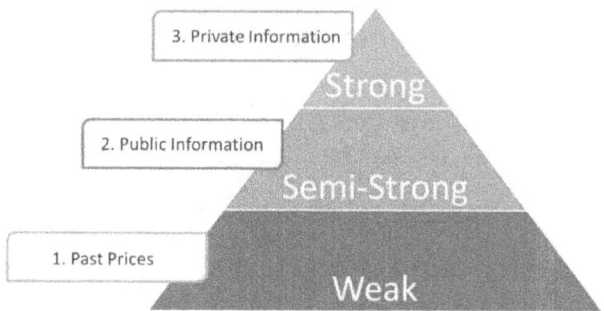

Weak Form EMH: Suggests that all past information is priced into securities. Fundamental analysis of securities can provide an investor with information to produce returns above market averages in the short term, but there are no "patterns" that exist. Therefore, fundamental analysis does not provide long-term advantage and technical analysis will not work. Weak form EMH assumes that the current market price reflects all historical price information about a security's price. The argument for weak EMH is that all new price movements are unrelated to historical data. So, those who believe this theory think that all future share price movements cannot be predicted based on previous price moves – essentially, the market is completely unpredictable as explained in random walk theory.

If a market is deemed to be 'weak-form efficient', it would mean that no correlation exists between historical prices and successive prices. This would mean that fundamental analysis might help traders to gather information and produce above-average returns, but that no patterns exist within price charts – therefore technical analysis is an inefficient methodology for entering and exiting weak-form efficient markets.

Semi-Strong Form EMH: Implies that neither fundamental analysis nor technical analysis can provide an advantage for an investor and that new information is instantly priced in to securities. Proponents of semi-strong form EMH believe that all publicly available information is factored into the market price. The theory states that the study of this information – which could include company balance sheets and historical share prices – could not result in oversized results.

A semi-strong form efficient market would mean that neither fundamental nor technical analysis could provide advantageous information, as all new information is instantly priced into the market. Semi-strong EMH believes that only those with privately held information could hold an advantage.

Those who believe semi-strong form EMH would question the need for a large portion of financial services, such as analysts and investment researchers.

Strong Form EMH: Says that all information, both public and private, is priced into stocks and that no investor can gain advantage over the market as a whole. Strong Form EMH does not say some investors or money managers are incapable of capturing abnormally high returns because that there are always outliers included in the averages. Strong form EMH states that all available information, both public and private, is priced into the price of a security. This would mean that no investor would consistently be able to beat the market as a whole, but that some individuals might make abnormal returns on occasion.

Strong form EMH assumes that the market is perfect, and so the only way an individual could make an excessive return is by using insider information. Both technical and fundamental analysis would be rendered moot, as neither could provide advantageous information.

For example, if everyone starts moving in one direction, it's normal for an investor to follow, even if there is not a rational reason for it.

If EMT were true then how do we explain these results?

Partnership	Period	Return	Market Return
Buffett Partnership, Ltd	1957–1969	29.50%	7.40%
Charles Munger, Ltd	1962–1975	19.80%	5.00%
Sequoia Fund, Inc	1970–1984	18.20%	10.00%
WJS Limited Partners	1956–1984	21.30%	8.40%

Prospect Theory

While economic rationality influenced other fields in the social sciences from the inside out, through Becker and the Chicago School, psychologists offered an outside-in reality check to prevailing economic thinking. Most notably, Amos Tversky and Daniel Kahneman published a number of papers that appeared to undermine ideas about human nature held by mainstream economics. They are perhaps best known for the development of prospect theory (Kahneman & Tversky, 1979), which shows that decisions are not always optimal. Our willingness to take risks is influenced by the way in which choices are framed, i.e. it is context-dependent. Have a look at the following classic decision problem:

Which of the following would you prefer?

A) A certain win of $250, versus

B) A 25% chance to win $1000 and a 75% chance to win nothing?

How about

C) A certain loss of $750, versus

D) A 75% chance to lose $1000 and a 25% chance to lose nothing?

Tversky and Kahneman's work shows that responses are different if choices are framed as a gain (1) or a loss (2). When faced with the first type of decision, a greater proportion of people will opt for the riskless alternative A), while for the second problem people are more likely to choose the riskier D). This happens because we dislike losses more than we like an equivalent gain: Giving something up is more painful than the pleasure we derive from receiving it.

Mental Accounting

The economist Richard Thaler, a keen observer of human behavior and founder of behavioral economics, was inspired by Kahneman & Tversky's work (see Thaler, 2015, for a summary). Thaler coined the concept of mental accounting. According to Thaler, people think of value in relative rather than absolute terms. They derive pleasure not just from an object's value, but also the quality of the deal – its transaction utility (Thaler, 1985). In addition, humans often fail to fully consider opportunity costs (tradeoffs) and are susceptible to the sunk cost fallacy.

Why are people willing to spend more when they pay with a credit card than cash (Prelec & Simester, 2001)? Why would more individuals spend $10 on a theatre ticket if they had just lost a $10 bill than if they had to replace a lost ticket worth $10 (Kahneman & Tversky, 1984)? Why are people more likely to spend a small inheritance and invest a large one (Thaler, 1985)?

According to the theory of mental accounting, people treat money differently, depending on factors such as the money's origin and intended use, rather than thinking of it in terms of the "bottom line" as in formal accounting (Thaler, 1999). An important term underlying the theory is fungibility, the fact that all money is interchangable and has no labels. In mental accounting, people treat assets as less fungible than they really are. Even seasoned investors are susceptible to this bias when they view recent gains as disposable "house money" (Thaler & Johnson, 1990) that can be used in high-risk investments. In doing so, they make decisions on each mental account separately, losing out the big picture of the portfolio.

Consumers' tendency to work with mental accounts is reflected in various domains of applied behavioral science, especially in the financial services industry. Examples include banks offering multiple accounts with savings goal labels, which make mental accounting more explicit, as well as third-party services that provide consumers with aggregate financial information across different financial institutions (Zhang & Sussman, 2018).

Another concept related to mental accounting captures the fact that people don't like to spend money. We experience pain of paying (Zellermayer, 1996), because we are loss averse. The pain of paying plays an important role in consumer self-regulation to keep spending in check (Prelec & Loewenstein, 1998). This pain is thought to be reduced in credit card purchases, because plastic is less tangible than cash, the depletion of resources (money) is less visible and payment is deferred. Different types of people experience different levels of pain of paying, which can affect spending decisions. Tightwads, for instance, experience more of this pain than spendthrifts. As a result, tightwads are particularly sensitive to marketing contexts that make spending less painful (Rick, 2018). Example Tax Refunds. ,Birthday Money, Bonuses., "Safety Capital" Lottery Winnings.

Loss aversion

Loss aversion is an important concept associated with prospect theory and is encapsulated in the expression "losses loom larger than gains" (Kahneman & Tversky, 1979). It is thought that the pain of losing is psychologically about twice as powerful as the pleasure of gaining. People are more willing to take risks (or behave dishonestly; e.g. Schindler & Pfattheicher, 2016) to avoid a loss than to make a gain. Loss aversion has been used to explain the endowment effect and sunk cost fallacy, and it may also play a role in the status quo bias. In other words, losing something (an amount of money, an item, etc.) feels worse than gaining the same thing. It is a simple, but powerful bias that is encapsulated in the expression "losses loom larger than gains" (Kahneman & Tversky, 1979).

For example, what would you choose: to receive a guaranteed payment of $900 or take a 90% chance of winning $1000 (and a 10% chance of winning 0)? Most people would decide to avoid the risk and take the

$900, although the expected outcome is the same in both cases. However, if I asked you to choose between losing $900 and take a 90% chance of losing $1000, it is more likely that would probably prefer the second option (with the 90% chance of losing $1000) and thus engage in the risk-seeking behaviour in the hope to avoid the loss.

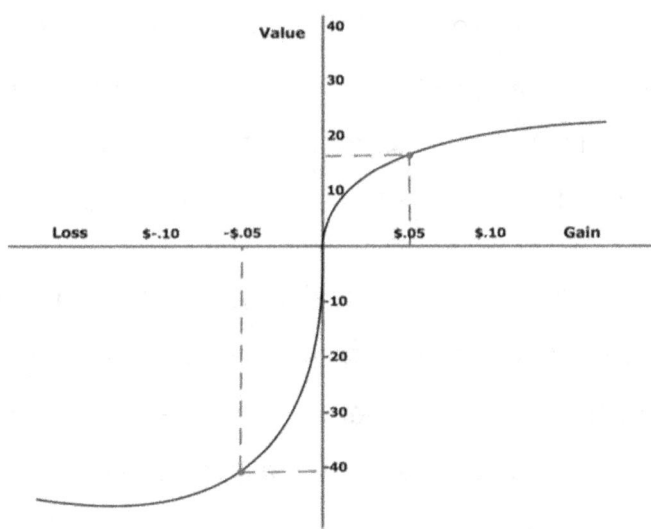

Framing effect

The framing effect is a cognitive bias where people decide on options based on whether the options are presented with positive or negative connotations; e.g. as a loss or as a gain.

People tend to avoid risk when a positive frame is presented but seek risks when a negative frame is presented. Gain and loss are defined in the scenario as descriptions of outcomes (e.g., lives lost or saved, disease patients treated and not treated, etc.).

The framing effect has consistently proven to be one of the strongest biases in decision making. The ways in which framing can be used are nearly unlimited; from emotional appeals to social pressure to priming.

When a positive frame is presented people are more likely to avoid risks, but will be risk-seeking when a negative frame is presented. Especially important to note is that the effect seems to increase with age, which is important when designing health and financial policies.

Which one of these products would you pick: A '95% effective' Medicine or a '5% failure' Medicine? '80% lean' ground chicken or '20%' fat ground chicken? Most people would be more likely to choose the first option in both cases, even though the two choices are identical.

FROZEN YOGURT
CONTAIN 20 % FAT

FROZEN YOGURT
80 % FAT FREE

Regret Aversion

When people fear that their decision will turn out to be wrong in hindsight, they exhibit regret aversion. Regret-averse people may fear the consequences of both errors of omission (e.g. not buying the right investment property) and commission (e.g. buying the wrong investment property) (Seiler et al., 2008). The effect of anticipated regret is particularly well-studied in the domain of health, such as people's decisions about medical treatments. A meta-analysis in this area suggests that anticipated regret is a better predictor of intentions and behaviour than other kinds of anticipated negative emotions and evaluations of risk (Brewer et al., 2016). (See also loss aversion, status quo bias, sunk cost fallacy, information avoidance, and action bias)

When picking stocks, one should consider the likelihood of it rising and falling, and the harm and gain that each would cause. What most people do is different. They consider how bad it would feel if the stock did as poorly as they could imagine it doing, and attempt to minimize that feeling. This leads to incorrectly risk-averse strategies.

Ambiguity Aversion

Ambiguity aversion is a preference for known risks over unknown risks. An ambiguity-averse individual would rather choose an alternative where the probability distribution of the outcomes is known over one where the probabilities are unknown. This behaviour was first introduced through the Ellsberg paradox (people prefer to bet on the outcome of an urn with 50 red and 50 blue balls rather than to bet on one with 100 total balls but for which the number of blue or red balls is unknown.

There are two categories of imperfectly predictable events between which choices must be made: risky and ambiguous events (also known as Knightian uncertainty). Risky events have a known probability distribution over outcomes while in ambiguous events the probability distribution is not known. The reaction is behavioral and still being formalized. Ambiguity aversion can be used to explain incomplete contracts, volatility in stock markets, and selective abstention in elections (Ghirardato & Marinacci, 2001).

The distinction between ambiguity aversion and risk aversion is important but subtle. Risk aversion comes from a situation where a probability can be assigned to each possible outcome of a situation and it is defined by the preference between a risky alternative and its expected value. Ambiguity aversion applies to a situation when the probabilities of outcomes are unknown (Epstein 1999) and it is defined through the preference between risky and ambiguous alternatives, after controlling for preferences over risk.

Using the traditional two-urn Ellsberg choice, urn A contains 50 red balls and 50 blue balls while urn B contains 100 total balls (either red or blue) but the number of each is unknown. An individual who prefers a certain payoff strictly smaller than $10 over a bet that pays $20 if the colour of a ball drawn from urn A is guessed correctly and $0 otherwise is said to be risk averse but nothing can be said about her preferences over ambiguity. On the other hand, an individual who strictly prefers that same bet if the ball is drawn from urn A over the case where the ball is drawn from urn B is said to be ambiguity averse but not necessarily risk averse.

A real world consequence of increased ambiguity aversion is the increased demand for insurance because the general public are averse to the unknown events that will affect their lives and property (Alary, Treich, and Gollier 2010).

Cognitive Bias

A cognitive bias is a systematic error in thinking that affects the decisions and judgments that people make. Some of these biases are related to memory. The way you remember an event may be biased for a number of reasons and that in turn can lead to biased thinking and decision-making. Other cognitive biases might be related to problems with attention. Since attention is a limited resource, people have to be selective about what they pay attention to in the world around them. Because of this, subtle biases can creep in and influence the way you see and think about the world.

A cognitive bias is a type of error in thinking that occurs when people are processing and interpreting information in the world around them. The human brain is powerful but subject to limitations. Cognitive biases are often a result of your brain's attempt to simplify information processing. They are rules of thumb that help you make sense of the world and reach decisions with relative speed.

When you are making judgments and decisions about the world around you, you like to think that you are objective, logical, and capable of taking in and evaluating all the information that is available to you. Unfortunately, these biases sometimes trip us up, leading to poor decisions and bad judgments.

If you had to think about every possible option when making a decision, it would probably take a lot of time to make even the simplest choice. Because of the sheer complexity of the world around you and the amount of information in the environment, it is necessary sometimes to rely on some mental shortcuts that allow you to act quickly.

Cognitive biases can be caused by a number of different things, but it is these mental shortcuts, known as heuristics, that often play a major contributing role. While they can often be surprisingly accurate, they can also lead to errors in thinking. Social pressures, individual motivations, emotions, and limits on the mind's ability to process information can also contribute to these biases.

These biases are not necessarily all bad, however. Psychologists believe that many of these biases serve an adaptive purpose—they allow us to reach decisions quickly. This can be vital if we are facing a dangerous or threatening situation. If you are walking down a dark alley and spot a dark shadow that seems to be following you, a cognitive bias might lead you to assume that it is a mugger and that you need to exit the alley as quickly as possible. The dark shadow may have simply been caused by a flag waving in the breeze, but relying on mental shortcuts can often get you out of the way of danger in situations where decisions need to be made quickly.

Types of Bias:

Confirmation Bias: This is favoring information that conforms to your existing beliefs and discounting evidence that does not conform. Good news for stock to go up, we might buy the stock but ignore the truth of the news is correct or not.

Availability Heuristic: This is placing greater value on information that comes to your mind quickly. You give greater credence to this information and tend to overestimate the probability and likelihood of similar things happening in the future.

Halo Effect: Your overall impression of a person influences how you feel and think about his or her character. This especially applies to physical attractiveness influencing how you rate their other qualities.

Self-Serving Bias: This is the tendency to blame external forces when bad things happen and give you credit when good things happen. When you win a poker hand it is due to your skill at reading the other players and knowing the odds, while when you lose it is due to getting dealt a poor hand.

Attentional Bias: This is the tendency to pay attention to some things while simultaneously ignoring others. When making a decision on which car to buy, you may pay attention to the look and feel of the exterior and interior, but ignore the safety record and gas mileage.

Actor-Observer Bias: This is the tendency to attribute your own actions to external causes while attributing other people's behaviours to internal causes. You attribute your high cholesterol level to genetics while you consider others to have a high level due to poor diet and lack of exercise.

Functional Fixedness: This is the tendency to see objects as only working in a particular way. If you don't have a hammer, you never consider that a big wrench can also be used to drive a nail into the wall. You may think you don't need thumbtacks because you have no corkboard on which to tack things, but not consider their other uses. This could extend to people's functions, such as not realizing a personal assistant has skills to be in a leadership role.

Anchoring Bias: This is the tendency to rely too heavily on the very first piece of information you learn. If you learn the average price for a car is a certain value, you will think any amount below that is a good deal, perhaps not searching for better deals. You can use this bias to set the expectations of others by putting the first information on the table for consideration. Stock which has fallen from a 52 week high investor like such stock buys again.

Misinformation Effect: This is the tendency for post-event information to interfere with the memory of the original event. It is easy to have your memory influenced by what you hear about the event from others. Knowledge of this effect has led to a mistrust of eyewitness information.

False Consensus Effect: This is the tendency to overestimate how much other people agree with you.

Optimism Bias: This bias leads you to believe that you are less likely to suffer from misfortune and more likely to attain success than your peers.

The Dunning-Kruger Effect: This is when people believe that they are smarter and more capable than they really are when they can't recognize their own incompetence.

Gambler's Fallacy: The most famous example of Gambler's Fallacy occurred at the Monte Carlo casino in Las Vegas in 1913. The roulette wheel's ball had fallen on black several times in a row. This led people to believe that it would fall on red soon and they started pushing their chips, betting that the ball would fall in a red square on the next roulette wheel turn. The ball fell on the red square after 27 turns. Accounts state that millions of dollars had been lost by then. This line of thinking in a Gambler's Fallacy or Monte Carlo Fallacy represents an inaccurate understanding of probability. This concept can apply to investing. Some investors liquidate a position after it has gone up after a long series of trading sessions. They do so because they erroneously believe that because of the string of successive gains, the position is now much more likely to decline.

certain value, you will think any amount below that is a good deal, perhaps not searching for better deals. You can use this bias to set the expectations of others by putting the first information on the table for consideration. Stock which has fallen from a 52 week high investor like such stock buys again.

Misinformation Effect: This is the tendency for post-event information to interfere with the memory of the original event. It is easy to have your memory influenced by what you hear about the event from others. Knowledge of this effect has led to a mistrust of eyewitness information.

False Consensus Effect: This is the tendency to overestimate how much other people agree with you.

Optimism Bias: This bias leads you to believe that you are less likely to suffer from misfortune and more likely to attain success than your peers.

The Dunning-Kruger Effect: This is when people believe that they are smarter and more capable than they really are when they can't recognize their own incompetence.

Gambler's Fallacy: The most famous example of Gambler's Fallacy occurred at the Monte Carlo casino in Las Vegas in 1913. The roulette wheel's ball had fallen on black several times in a row. This led people to believe that it would fall on red soon and they started pushing their chips, betting that the ball would fall in a red square on the next roulette wheel turn. The ball fell on the red square after 27 turns. Accounts state that millions of dollars had been lost by then. This line of thinking in a Gambler's Fallacy or Monte Carlo Fallacy represents an inaccurate understanding of probability. This concept can apply to investing. Some investors liquidate a position after it has gone up after a long series of trading sessions. They do so because they erroneously believe that because of the string of successive gains, the position is now much more likely to decline.

Overcoming Behavioral Finance Issues

There are ways to overcome negative behavioral tendencies in relation to investing. Here are some strategies you can use to guard against biases.

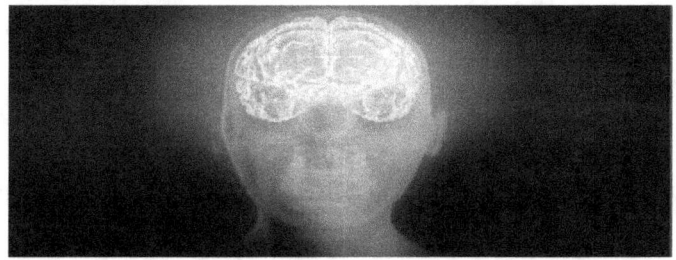

There are two approaches to decision-making:

- Reflexive – Going with your gut, which is effortless, automatic and, in fact, is our default option.

- Reflective – Logical and methodical, but requires effort to engage in actively.

Relying on reflexive decision-making makes us more prone to deceptive biases and emotional and social influences. Establishing logical decision-making processes can help protect you from such errors.

Get yourself focused on the process rather than the outcome. If you're advising others, try to encourage the people you're advising to think about the process rather than just the possible outcomes. Focusing on the process will lead to better decisions because the process helps you engage in reflective decision-making.

www.ingramcontent.com/pod-product-compliance
Lightning Source LLC
Chambersburg PA
CBHW071354210526
45465CB00001B/87